2939?

Collecting Himself

JAMES THURBER
ON WRITING AND WRITERS,
HUMOR AND HIMSELF

Books by James Thurber

Thurber and Company
Credos and Curios
Lanterns and Lances
The Years with Ross
Alarms and Diversions
The Wonderful O
Further Fables for Our Time
Thurber's Dogs
Thurber Country
The Thurber Album
The 13 Clocks
The Beast in Me and Other Animals
The White Deer
The Thurber Carnival
The Great Quillow
Men, Women and Dogs
Many Moons
My World—and Welcome to It
Fables for Our Time and Famous Poems Illustrated
The Last Flower
Let Your Mind Alone! and Other More or Less Inspirational Pieces
The Middle-Aged Man on the Flying Trapeze
My Life and Hard Times
The Seal in the Bedroom and Other Predicaments
The Owl in the Attic and Other Perplexities
Is Sex Necessary? or Why You Feel the Way You Do
(with E. B. White)

PLAY

The Male Animal
(with Elliott Nugent)

REVUE

A Thurber Carnival

LETTERS

Selected Letters of James Thurber

Collecting Himself

JAMES THURBER
ON WRITING AND WRITERS,
HUMOR AND HIMSELF

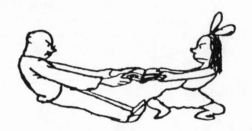

Michael J. Rosen, Editor

1817

HARPER & ROW, PUBLISHERS, New York
GRAND RAPIDS, PHILADELPHIA, ST. LOUIS, SAN FRANCISCO
LONDON, SINGAPORE, SYDNEY, TOKYO, TORONTO

Designed by Barbara DuPree Knowles

LIBRARY OF CONGRESS CATALOGING-IN-PUBLICATION DATA

Thurber, James, 1894–1961.
  [Selections. 1989]
  Collecting himself: James Thurber on writing and writers,
humad and himself/Michael J. Rosen, editor—1st ed.
    p. cm.
  ISBN 0-06-016135-3
  I. Rosen, Michael J., 1954– . II. Title.
PS3539.H94A6   1989
818'.5209—dc20   89-45062

89 90 91 92 93 CC/HC 10 9 8 7 6 5 4 3 2

Contents

———

BELLES LETTRES AND ME
Thurber at Large in the Writers' Community

CONTENTS

ix

CONTENTS

CONTENTS

Acknowledgments

The reconsideration of James Thurber's uncollected work continues to be the engaging, productive, felicitious enterprise it is because four important sources have contributed to my understanding of Thurber's work and afforded me occasions to express that engagement. With enormous gratitude and a flush of pride, I extend my appreciation here to Rosemary Thurber, who, beyond the individual permissions for each work and drawing in the collection, has permitted me the honor of working with the Thurber estate in such an equitable, respectful, well-humored manner; to The Thurber House's board members and its executive director, Donn Vickers, who have afforded me a work environment that values and supports my own personal and professional growth; to Robert Tibbetts at the Division of Rare Books and Manuscripts of The Ohio State University Special Collections, whose facility with and knowledge of Thurber brought the libraries' archives and Thurber's vast bibliography within my reach; and last, to Mark Svede and the other people of my extended family for the outside opinions on all kinds of queries and readings, as well as for the inside acceptances of my working temperaments and hours.

at 48, going on
49, I am getting along
as well as might be
expected, seeing a trifle
better. I draw now
with a Zeiss loop,
and look like a
welder from Mars

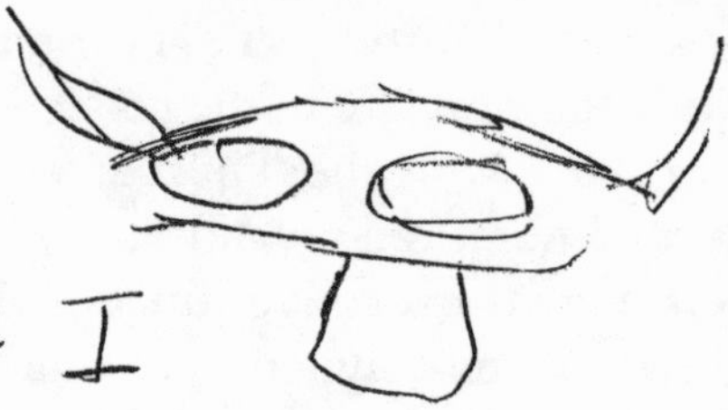

FIG I

FIG I shows the
wrong way to wear
a Zeiss loop — the
nose should be centered

EDITOR'S NOTE: The above passage from a letter to Herman and Dorothy Miller, dated May 28, 1943, reads: "At 48, going on 49, I am getting along as well as might be expected, seeing a trifle better. I draw now with a Zeiss loop, and look like a welder from Mars. Fig. I shows the wrong way to wear a Zeiss loop—the nose should be centered."

Preface

When visitors come to The Thurber House, the home where Jim and his family resided during his college years, 1913 to 1917, the home that eventually shaped many of the tales in *My Life and Hard Times,* they want to discover the familiar stories and drawings preserved, somehow, along with the oiled pine floors where Thurber's bull terrier Rex slept, among the fixtures that—still?—leak electricity. They want to sound out songs from Thurber's early Scarlet Mask musicals on a piano whose price in the Sears Roebuck catalogue of the times was about the cost of a decent typing chair today. They hope to sight Thurber's youthful inspirations haunting the house in cahoots with the famous ghost that got in.

Those who remember how Thurber's progressing blindness prompted him to draw with a black crayon on poster-sized paper or with white chalk on black paper ask to try on his Zeiss loop, that headband of magnifying lenses Thurber wore to accomplish those last drawings. Not normally a part of the tour, the loop creates a frightening topography of the wrinkles and hairs on a hand held five inches from its lenses. (See Thurber's own Fig. I.) They want to sniff the cologne in the monogrammed bottle from Dunhill's, open Thurber's leather briefcase, decipher a framed canary page of Thurber's enormous, barely legible script. (Consider, too, the handwriting in the excerpted letter.) The boldest visitors will tentatively depress the space bar on the Underwood #5 typewriter on which Thurber composed many of the stories and casuals for *The New Yorker.*

We can show visitors these things. The docents can read aloud from the Columbustown stories. But we fall short, of course, in our attempts to show Thurber becoming a writer, discovering his particular materials and genius, and honing the forms that would best convey his bristling compound of hard-earned, soft-hearted sympathy for this wayward, worrisome, and often unwelcoming world. We're unable to display how he came to make his work, his art, his *labor,* out of these very surroundings and their biographical circumstances.

Collecting Himself begins to address this subtler curiosity that a reader, a literary pilgrim, might possess about James Thurber. Were Thurber alive, were he a part of our guest writers series at The Thurber House, the reader's interest would probably be articulated with the same general questions our audience members invariably pose to visiting contemporary writers: (1) "What are your 'conditions' for writing?" (i.e., What are your ideal hours, surroundings, and paraphernalia?); (2) "What were your influences?" (i.e., Who did you read, what did you study, and where did you gather material?); and (3) "What are you reading now?" (i.e., Who do you admire, who should I be reading, do you agree that so and so is over-/under-rated?). The audience members also pose questions less specific to literary life, questions that might be asked of the writer-as-correspondent—or better, respondent: a worldly attaché whose views on political embroilments and cultural phenomena they would like to hear expressed with the same fluency and perspicuity with which the writer's published work has been enjoyed.

In lieu of a casual evening with the author, *Collecting Himself* should begin to respond to those questions about James Thurber as a composite creature: reader, writer, cartoonist, critic, journalist, respondent, and above all (or through it all) an unclassifiable Thurber—a beast that readers around the world have adopted, read, taught, and shared like no other figure in the natural history of pictures and letters.

By "collecting himself," I mean something akin to "composing himself," and I submit that the present compilation will show something of Thurber's literary composition: a rare admixture of abandon, conscientiousness, curiosity, uneasiness, urgency, pedantry, confabulation, wiliness—so many conflicting qualities that his prose recognized rather than reconciled. Arranged primarily by theme rather than by chronology or genre, the pieces here show a man *learning*—as in the other meaning of "to collect"—to reorient himself, as if after some unsettling personal or public confrontation. It should be no surprise that humor is Thurber's prevailing mode of equilibrium, that single form that has it both ways: admits *and* refutes; calls into question *and* then answers. It should also be no surprise that men, women, dogs, and other reputable distractions play important parts in Thurber's balancing act, however writerly or literary the table of contents might appear.

The work included in *Collecting Himself* has never appeared in a book by James Thurber. With few exceptions—notably those that have never appeared in print before—the writings, captioned drawings, and spot illustrations enjoyed a one-time appearance in a magazine or a newspaper or as a part of another author's book.

While Thurber included some of his best pieces on his own work and reading in his many anthologies, the convening, in a single volume, of the many he did not choose presents a creative coherence that has never before emerged in all of its passion and dispassion, flippancy and contempt, awe and eloquence. Writing of others' works, Thurber discovered the values that he would either appreciate or disdain in his own work. By plotting the points that he makes in reference to others (x=here, a genuine concern; y=there, a round of unreserved applause, or a dismissive swipe, or a raised eyebrow), a figure of Thurber's own accomplishment can be traced. This is, I believe, what we mean by a writer's style: the working solution of those qualities that a writer holds to and holds off simultaneously.

I have tried to employ Thurber's own instincts for anthologizing by mixing various kinds of work—article, essay, review, cartoon, parody—into a volume that can be read from cover to cover. Unless one pruned or burnished each piece, there is no escaping the eclectic, momentum-gathering, at-large-and-getting-larger ways of Thurber's energetic considerations. All that's left to us is relishing. Nonetheless, I have imposed a design, intending it to be the sort that Robert Frost commended when he spoke of a poem moving under the weight of its own making "like a block of ice on a hot stove." *Collecting Himself* should glide with the passionate heat and portentous weight of humor through Thurber's working thoughts on his creative processes, on the climate for humor writing and playwriting, on the inspirations for his drawings, on the works of his contemporaries and on contemporary society.

Perhaps any composite recollection of a writer is as cheerfully skewed as the seance in Thurber's famous drawing in which the medium announces, "I can't get in touch with your uncle, but there's a horse here that wants to say hello." But perhaps we can yet make out a ghostlike image of James Thurber from the imitations, parodies, letters, "playlets," apologies, editorials, cartoons, and tributes that Thurber wrote in the nearly fifty-year period contained here.

The texts are as free from editorial intervention as possible; a footnote is supplied only when a reader might otherwise be distracted by a reference or allusion. The Notes section at the end of the book provides relevant contextual annotations as well as information about where and when each piece was originally published.

The greatest attrition in compiling this book occurred among pieces where the requisite editorial framework would have weakened the effective punch of the writing. Primarily, these were writings centered on an individual who has been displaced from our current attention and memory or reviews and prefaces of books outside our familiar canon that Thurber did not feel compelled to summarize or gloss himself.

I have supplied an additional structure to coalesce excerpts from some of Thurber's interviews and commentaries. As he enjoyed continual popularity from works as wide-ranging as his *Fables,* his revue *A Thurber Carnival,* and his various published collections, Thurber agreed to a staggering number of formal and informal, written and oral, brief and extended interviews. In pieces that span some thirty years of questions and answers, the interviewers, too, shared but a few basic questions, focusing on his early years, his eyes, his method of drawing, his tactics in writing, his relationship to Harold Ross or E. B. White, his true thoughts on dogs and women. In London during 1958, having been "assiduously solicited by press, TV, and radio on everything from the future of humor in the nuclear age to the sex life of frustrated bloodhounds," Thurber told Eddy Gilmore, "I'm getting tired of hearing about myself over here." In the AP story of August 10, Gilmore added, "But he said it softly. And almost as if he felt he was to blame for getting tired of himself."

Clearly, the whole popularizing and intrusive phenomenon, combined with Thurber's extraordinary memory, helped him to polish his multifarious experience and considerable opinions into anecdotes, soliloquies, spiels, and aphorisms. These selected pieces form a loose monologue that appears throughout the book in sections called "Speaking of . . ." I have intended these fragments to derive further substantiation from the book's calculated, revised expressions, in hopes of allaying what I suspect would have been stern reservations on Thurber's part. Despite his generosity with the media, he was wary of dangers created by the ease of oral composition. After a lengthy interview with Harvey Brandon, he sent his misgivings in a three-page, single-spaced letter to Brandon:

> In the watches of the night I began remembering recent verbal assaults I have made, when in a bad mood, upon the craze for interviews. My opposition lies in the fact that offhand answers have little value or grace of expression, and that such oral give and take helps to perpetuate the decline of the English language in my country and yours [England]. . . . While lying around dawn this morning I began polishing some of the things I told you. Since I rewrite everything all the way through from five to twenty times, it is hard for me to think of my conversational replies being used as my final considered opinions and judgments.

(According to Brandon, both participants finally conceded that the taped conversation was the better. [BRANDON])

The last question to which any posthumous volume might be subjected is, "Why didn't the author collect these pieces before?" In Thurber's specific case, more than the usual number of factors combine to provide the always unsatisfactory answer.

But before any supererogation on my part, I should note that Thurber shot several, somewhat parting, glances at his future executor's work. In "The Notebooks of James Thurber," published posthumously in *Credos and Curios*, Thurber pokes among his own "memoranda and memorabilia":

> What I came up with presents a very dark picture indeed, complete with at least seven major deterrents [to a "serious literary

executor"]: persistent illegibility, paucity of material, triviality of content, ambiguity of meaning, facetious approach, preponderance of juvenilia, and exasperating abbreviation.

Thurber described the executor himself with no less delicacy, suspecting that he

> will hang around your house, known as "the estate," for at least a year, mousing through voluminous papers, collating and annotating, drinking your Scotch with your widow, and sometimes, in the end, marrying your daughter.
>
> There is also the disturbing chance that your executor . . . may stumble on the Figure in the Carpet. . . . That is, he may adduce from the notebooks dubious internal evidence supporting the theory that you were . . .

well, various things. In what follows I hope that in my role as mere editor, I have escaped Thurber's prefiguring as I propose my reasons for selecting what Thurber himself never selected, and I make public my genuine appreciation of—not my marital intentions toward—Rosemary Thurber, James's executrix and daughter.

The simplest answer and, admittedly, the most daunting to an editor is that Thurber didn't like the specific writing. I hope, of the nearly fifty pieces included here, this reason applies to very few, but I risk saying that a writer's own estimation of a given piece at a given time isn't necessarily a judgment of its actual quality. Moreover, humorous writing, the sort of nervy, unnerved journalism that Thurber fashioned, is, perhaps, all the more inscrutable within the span of one's own life. The problem could be—Thurber himself discusses this danger in the "Speaking of Humor . . ." section—that the humor of a piece didn't age well. It could also be, I offer, that it didn't age long enough. As we near the twenty-first century, we can look at a Thurber parody from the 1930s, for example, and regard it as a genuine representative of a period—both the cultural period and the period of Thurber's own writing. (Certainly, the latter perspective would tax an author's humility beyond the bounds of critical assessment.) The view from the 1940s—whether from that of a reader or that of the anthologizing eye of the author himself—might have seen this same parody as outdated, not timely enough, or rendered trite by the popularity of lesser versions by subsequent practitioners. The view from the 1950s might have seen this same piece as "nostalgic," too familiar to be rediscovered and yet too remote to be fully recognizable. But now, nearly thirty years after Thurber's death and fifty years after our 1930s example was first published, the humor of the writing can be seen for exactly what it was; in the overwhelming number of cases, we can also see the humor for what it is today.

Other simpler answers for Thurber's omissions, answers more frequently shared by other authors, include the possibility that a given writing was too closely related to another feature in a particular book or, conversely, that it was not related enough to fit that book's theme. And another: that Thurber felt the piece—say, a review or an introduction—was in the service of another writer's work, not really something he wanted to claim for his own general readership.

The more complicated, Thurber-specific reasons arise from his progressive blindness, the many eye surgeries, and the strain of related physiological and psychological illnesses, which often physically kept Thurber from writing, but always kept his writing physically from him. True, Thurber could compose in his head, holding up to 2,000 words, he often boasted; he could fit a dozen handwritten words on one sheet of paper and thereby construct a casual (a brief essay for "Talk of the Town" in *The New Yorker*) the size of a novel; he would dictate to his secretaries and to his wife, Helen, and he could readily respond to someone reading a piece back to him—but it is implausible to imagine Thurber in full possession of the enormous body of his uncollected work. Even allowing Thurber his extremely retentive memory, how many projects—the all-but-finished, the to-be-revised, the rejected-and-to-be-reconsidered, the finished-and-awaiting-a-place, and so on—could he command? And we must remember that on top of previous work or reworking, Thurber continued to write with an obsessive, manic charge (even if only his prolific, often prodigious, correspondence) through all but his most compromised days.

Indeed, there were always several new projects in progress—plays that never reached an acting script, a novel that preoccupied a decade, each month's projected stories, casuals, or essays. Despite the heroic labors of his wife, friends, or secretaries, it is highly likely that an individual piece was overlooked, displaced, or forgotten in the heat of an especially volatile project; it is certain that several were prevented from receiving the many extensive revisions that Thurber imposed on his work. Yet it is also amazing—and it is with this note of confidence that my guesswork concludes—that Thurber managed to execute as much as he did and that there remain for present readers the pleasures of both the vintage and the novelty of his work.

Michael J. Rosen

Courting the Muse

THURBER AT WORK

Speaking of His Own Writing . . .

I admire the person who can write it right off. Mencken once said that a person who thinks clearly can write well. But I don't think clearly—too many thoughts bump into one another. Trains of thought run on a track of the Central Nervous System—the New York Central Nervous System, to make it worse. [LIFE]

* * *

Hervey Allen, you know, the author of the big best-seller *Anthony Adverse,* seriously told a friend of mine who was working on a biographical piece on Allen that he could close his eyes, lie down on a bed, and hear the voices of his ancestors. Furthermore, there was some sort of angel-like creature that danced along his pen while he was writing. He wasn't balmy by any means. He just felt he was in communication with some sort of metaphysical recorder. So you see the novelists have all the luck. I never knew a humorist who got any help from his ancestors. [PARIS]

* * *

Still, the act of writing is either something the writer dreads or actually likes, and I actually like it. Even re-writing's fun. You're getting somewhere, whether it seems to move or not. I remember

EDITOR'S NOTE: For the source of each interview or article, please see the Notes on pages 249–250, matching the key word at the end of each excerpt with the list's respective entry.

Elliot Paul and I used to argue about re-writing back in 1925 when we both worked for the *Chicago Tribune* in Paris. It was his conviction you should leave the story as it came out of the typewriter, no changes. Naturally, he worked fast. Three novels he could turn out, each written in three weeks' time. [PARIS]

* * *

[Georges] Simenon, who can write four hundred times as fast as we can, happened to drop in yesterday with my English publisher, Hamish Hamilton. Fastest writers I know are Sally Benson and John O'Hara. O'Hara, like me, is no good at plotting in advance, but his only revising, even of novels, is what he calls "pencil work," a minor change here and there in final rereading. When you consider that *Appointment in Samarra* was done like that, it makes you think that the boy is a genius. One thing is sure, a genius, by definition, doesn't have to go over and over his stuff. [COWLEY]

* * *

I draw in the south light of a glassed-in porch and write in a bedroom of my house, a mile from Cornwall Plains, Connecticut, and three hours from the Algonquin Hotel. I once worked in a well-lighted bathroom and have done drawings while riding on trains or lying down or sitting with friends in a restaurant. The Perfect Place to write a fairy tale is Bermuda, with its 1913 tranquility, and there I did "The Thirteen Clocks" last spring, a clock a week. For other stories all I need is a card table, anywhere, a hundred sharpened pencils, and a lot of yellow paper, since I use a thousand sheets a month, perhaps two hundred of them worth saving. [FALL AUTHOR]

* * *

[a first draft is] just for size. . . . That draft isn't any good; it isn't supposed to be; the whole purpose is to sketch out proportions. . . . I rarely have a very clear idea of where I'm going when I start. Just people and a situation. Then I fool around—writing and re-writing until the stuff jells. [GELDER]

JAMES THURBER

* * *

I used to be a writer who thought on the typewriter. My father had been with Underwood, and I knew how to typewrite by the time I was 6. Writers have wanted to run me out of town on a rail because I've said I like the physical business of writing on a typewriter. Now, I use a soft black pencil on yellow copy paper. I get about twenty words on a sheet. When I finish a short story it's about the size of a novel. I can't read those twenty words back. Fortunately, I have a good memory. . . . Usually I get from 500 to 1,500 words in my mind before I start writing. Also I have shifted from being an eye-writer to being an ear-writer. Mrs. Thurber can read my unreadable hand and reads what I've written back to me. [BREIT]

* * *

I often tell them [works-in-progress] at parties and places. And I write them there too. . . . I never quite know when I'm not writing. Sometimes my wife comes up to me at a party and says, "Dammit, Thurber, stop writing." She usually catches me in the middle of a paragraph. Or my daughter will look up from the dinner table and ask, "Is he sick?" "No," my wife says, "he's writing something." I have to do it that way on account of my eyes. I still write occasionally—in the proper sense of the word—using black crayon on yellow paper and getting perhaps twenty words to the page. My usual method, though, is to spend the mornings turning over the text in my mind. Then in the afternoon, between 2 and 5, I call in a secretary and dictate to her. [PARIS]

* * *

A blind man benefits by a lack of distractions. I remember sitting with Ross at a table in this restaurant. He picked up a bottle of Worcester-shire sauce and then threw it down, saying, "Goddammit, that's the 10,000th time I've read the label on this bottle." I told him, "God-dammit, Harold, that's because you're handicapped by vision."

The luckiest thing that can happen to a blind man is to have total recall. I first found out I had it in 1913, when I was in a psychology class at Ohio State. There were forty in the class, conducted by a Viennese professor named Weiss. He read a 1,000-word piece to us, and then told us to write down as much as we could remember. My score was 78 per cent, the next highest was 20. Three weeks later, he told us to write down as much as we could remember. This time my score was 50 percent, the next highest was 6. [DOLBIER]

* * *

Well, you know it's a nuisance—to have a memory like mine—as well as an advantage. It's . . . well . . . like a whore's top drawer. There's so much else in there that's junk . . . costume jewelry, unnecessary telephone numbers whose exchanges no longer exist. For instance, I can remember the birthday of anybody who's ever told me his birthday. Dorothy Parker—August 22nd, Lewis Gannett—October 3rd, Andy White—July 9th, Mrs. White—September 17th. I can go on with about 200. . . .

I don't have to do the sort of thing Fitzgerald did with *The Last Tycoon*—the voluminous, the tiny and meticulous notes, the long descriptions of character. I can keep all these things in my mind. I wouldn't have to write down "three roses in a vase," or something, or a man's middle name. Henry James dictated notes just the way that I write. His note-writing was part of the creative act, which is why his prefaces are so good. He dictated notes to see what it was that they might come to. [PARIS]

* * *

Helen is one of the greatest proofreaders, editors, and critics I've ever known. She's often rescued things I've thrown aside. And, if there's something she doesn't like, she pulls no punches. When I wrote "The Secret Life of Walter Mitty," I had a scene in which Mitty got between Hemingway and an opponent in a Stork Club brawl. Helen said that had to come out, that there should be nothing topical in the story. Well, you know how it is when your wife is right. You grouse around the house for a week, and then you follow her advice. [DOLBIER]

JAMES THURBER

* * *

I've never wanted to write a long work. Many writers feel a sense of frustration or something if they haven't, but I don't. . . . [Could the nature of humor impose a limit on a work's length?] Possibly. But brevity in any case—whether the word is supposed to be humorous or not—would seem to me to be desirable. Most of the books I like are short books: *The Red Badge of Courage, Turn of the Screw,* Conrad's short stories, *A Lost Lady,* Joseph Hergesheimer's *Wild Oranges,* Victoria Lincoln's *February Hill, The Great Gatsby* . . . you know Fitzgerald once wrote Thomas Wolfe: "You're a putter-inner and I'm a taker-outer." I stick with Fitzgerald. I don't believe, as Wolfe did, that you have to turn out a massive work before being judged a writer. Wolfe once told me at a cocktail party I didn't know what it was to be a writer. My wife, standing next to me, complained about that. "But my husband *is* a writer," she said. Wolfe was genuinely surprised. "He is?" he asked. "Why, all I ever see is that stuff of his in *The New Yorker.*" In other words he felt that prose under 5,000 words was certainly not the work of a writer . . . it was some kind of doodling in words. If you said you were a writer, he wanted to know where the books were, the great big long books. He was really genuine about that.

I was interested to see William Faulkner's list not so long ago of the five most important American authors of this century. According to him Wolfe was first, Faulkner second . . . let's see, now that Wolfe's dead that puts Faulkner up there in the lead, doesn't it? . . . Dos Passos third, then Hemingway, and finally Steinbeck. It's interesting that the first three are putter-inners. They write expansive novels. [PARIS]

* * *

And there's "The Train on Track 5." No, it's not a novel. I haven't written a novel, and don't plan to. It seems today that after youngsters get over the braces on their teeth, and then get through college, the next thing you hear their mother saying is, "Thank God, Tom or Harry has gotten over his first novel." No, "The Train on Track 5" is a satire on modern American life, done in terms of fairy tale and dream. I've been working on it, off and on, for some time, and it hasn't quite come right yet. My wife read a part of it aloud to some of our friends. I asked how it was received, and she said, "Well, some one kept making ugly sounds with their lips all through the reading. Me." [DOLBIER]

* * *

["The Spoodle" is] a sort of fairy tale that will run to about 12,000 words. . . . The story is placed in a country called Confusia. In it, everybody is supected of the wrong thing. One person has seen the spoodle, another has heard it, and a third has even tasted it. The prosecutor is sure that the spoodle is un-Confusian and has to find it. It he can't find one, the prosecutor says, he will have to build one. It's a satire on the Un-American Committee's worst confusions. Enough hasn't been said, by the way, about the term un-American. Imagine saying un-Persian or un-Belgian. [BREIT]

* * *

I once wanted to write a novel about Bernadette until that book came along. I have a theory about Bernadette and her vision. There are certain kinds of spots-before-the-eyes that take definite shapes. They are scientifically called phosphenes. I have a bright blue shape these days—though it used to be brighter. It's always there, but you have to look for it. At one time my phosphenes used to take the definite shape of the face of Herbert Hoover. Of course, it wouldn't make history. [BREIT]

* * *

Three sure-fire ones [best-sellers] I would like to write are: *How to Make Love and Money, How to Tell Your Blessings from Your Burdens,* and *How to Pass the Joneses at a Dogtrot.* [LIFE]

JAMES THURBER

"*Do you ever have fears that you may cease to be
before your pen has gleaned your teeming brain?*"

"He's giving Dorothy Thompson a piece of his mind."

JAMES THURBER

"Courting the Muse?"

COLLECTING HIMSELF

The Theory and Practice of Criticizing the Criticism of the Editing of New Yorker Articles

(WITH A LIGHTED CANDLE FOR WOLCOTT GIBBS)

1. When all things are equal, translucence in writing is more effective than transparency, just as glow is more revealing than glare (see E. B. White's "How to Tell a Major Poet from a Minor Poet," which was inspired by his wife's saying to him, "Why can't poets be more clear?").

2. The problem of the editor who is also a writer is considerable, as against that of the non-writing, or illiterate, editor, such as H. W. R. [Harold W. Ross]. Editing should be, especially in the case of old writers, a counselling rather than a collaborating task. The tendency of the writer-editor to collaborate is natural, but he should say to himself, "How can I help this writer to say it better in his own style?" and avoid "How can I show him how I would write it, if it were my piece?"

Malraux has said that form is the true expression of the artist and thus form cannot be changed without disaster to what the writer has to say.

JAMES THURBER

d "The Wood
editorial setup
y" the piece. I
re not allowed
as amended to
owed to shoot
re passed a law
hat I had to say
e collect phone
rom the wreck-
that fourteen-
of *New Yorker*

leal with dying
y usually turn
John] O'Hara
ught and then
his only works
e. Whether or
f rejection is a
America like
g off, that the
l not put on a
ong run. The
a lying-down
ot Pray Is Not

station as the
sked recently
otes, I stay
at "that"
sinking

pe casting a writer as in type
a tendency toward this as re-
of "uncharacteristic" and "un-
d twenty years ago that I be
ch got from Ross a "Dismiss it
book reviewer." Thurber had
and *Herald Tribune, The Nation,*
iew of Literature, the *Columbus*
Christian Science Monitor. This
ore book reviews.

's "It only leaves me fifty more"
It leaves me only fifty more." In
hio State musical comedy called
f says, "They is in jail" to which
n't get them both in on one is."
" the sheriff said.
y years in on one is, thus setting

ho can write, and write well, to
hor's was demonstrated when my
ed the day for his friends" was
kened the world etc." The word
ld, and the world cannot be dark-
rker, however eminent, because it
er, impersonal things. I anticipate
f *The New Yorker* will have domi-
iters so that the experience, beliefs,
e those of the writers.

ins an exchange of letters between him
n McNulty and it's worth reading [pages
old situation, my book reveals, was Bill
o preserved all the peculiar and inviolable
Gus Lobrano also helped and Ross used his
with them. I had been wrong in my fears

6. The piece of mine McNulty liked most was call
Duck" and it was the last piece of mine that the old
monkeyed with (1936) by sticking in a line to "clari
had a sentence that went something like this, "They
to shoot wood ducks in this state anymore." This w
read something like this, "Hunters haven't been all
wood ducks in this state since the Connecticut legislatu
in 1932 putting those birds on the protected list." Wl
about that cost *The New Yorker* seventeen dollars in on
call from Litchfield. Needless to say I saved the piece f
age of clarification. This clarification was on behalf o
year-old girl who is supposed to be a composite
readers. God help us all.

7. Editors must deal with rejections the way doctors d
persons, but doctors have an easier time, because the
the ordeal over to priests or parsons. The system with [
was to hand him a check for a piece that had been bo
slip him the piece that had been turned down, but tl
when two or more casuals have been submitted at on
not to explain to the author the why and wherefore o
moot point, and I understand the moot is dying out ir
the whooping crane. Some of us prefer to be told, bar
piece was not liked, but this doesn't mean that we wil
scene, nor does the scene really mean much in the l
writer who takes it lying down is what is known as
writer. (See Calvin Coolidge's "The Man Who Does N
a Praying Man.")

8. That "that" could easily become as serious an inf
commas that spread like black dandelions. When I was
to insert a "that" on behalf of style except in direct qu
awake writing such sentences as this. I consider that tl
worries us so much should be forgotten. Rats desert a
Thats infest a sinking magazine.

9. The writer's mind and the reader's eye must both b
and this is hard for the editor who is neither the writer n
Poetry solves these things so easily, and always has. Ta

JAMES THURBER

ple, this line from Catullus: "Vivamus, mea Lesbia, atque amemus" [*Carmina,* V, 1.1.]. The poet wrote it that way and the old Roman reader knew how to speak it aloud. This is the way one academic fellow fixed up the line in his book on Catullus: "Vivamus me(a), Lesbia, atqu(e) amemus." This is that old wood duck situation, with a distance of 2,000 years in between.

10. Henry James used more dependent clauses than anybody, in his long concentric sentences, but he also used few commas. He would have written it this way, "Tall dark and handsome." Since there is no dark that can be called tall dark, even the dark at the top of the stairs, there is no confusion.

My Ross book takes up the time that he decided, with White's approval, to punctuate the flag like this. "The red, white, and blue." I held out, futilely, for the red white and blue, and—oh, well, read the book.

In 1933 I wrote a casual which was rejected (it was serious and uncharacteristic) and it got lost. Later one editor said "they" wanted to see it again. This is known as delayed appreciation. In that piece I left the apostrophe out of every present participle on the ground that so many apostrophes are like so many fly specks. What is the matter with "I was lyin there and thinkin"? This simple solution was sheer revolution to Ross. It's worth thinking about, or thinkin.

11. I was sometimes not counselled enough by Lobrano, although he was 90 per cent right in not using a fine-tooth comb on my stuff. In those days the overall effect was sometimes lost sight of because of the concentration on words and phrases. As a result there are a dozen or more pieces of mine never included in books because I didn't consider them perfectly done. In *Alarms and Diversions* I rewrote, in part, three or four casuals, including "But It's Your Mother" and "And a Happy New Year."

The best example of my editing of my own stuff is worth looking up. It was a Talk interview I had with Jack Johnson way back in [Ralph] Ingersoll's time. I rewrote it for my book *The Beast in Me.* It might help a young editor of twenty to get the hang of rewrite, or at least to find out what was the matter with Thurber in Ingersoll's time.

12. I was not so much dismayed as amused when I discovered that the editors, in a jittery mood, or during certain phases of the moon, are "down readers." That is, they read the last word of each line from top to bottom and thus once encountered "Dixie cups." When an editor becomes a down reader, madness is just around the coroner. I am sure that this magazine's back files, if read down, instead of from left to right, would produce "girl laid," "trousers open," and God knows what other shocking atrocities. I always begin at the left with the opening word of the sentence and read toward the right and I recommend this method.

13. I have unfortunately lost a long letter sent me ten years ago by a professor of English in London, whose speciality is punctuation. He queried twelve or fifteen commas in twelve or fifteen different *New Yorker* pieces, finding them "unnecessary and disturbing." From one casual of mine he picked this sentence. "After dinner, the men moved into the living room." I explained to the professor that this was Ross's way of giving the men time to push back their chairs and stand up. There must, as we know, be a comma after every move, made by men, on this earth.

John Duncan Miller, formerly the *Times* of London man in Washington, said to me in 1955, "The biography of Harold Ross should be called 'The Century of the Comma Man.'"

14. I once heard a former football player say to his wife, "Let's skip it, shall we?" This was the only time I ever heard him use "shall," which we use too rarely and the English use too much. If you keep visiting London and staying there for months, you do begin using "shall" properly, and sometimes wrongly. The Thurber theory is that it fell into disrepute west of the Appalachians because it was considered, by guys like my old city editor Gus Kuehner, a schoolteacher's word, used only by men who flourished canes, drank tea, and ate ladyfingers. It can't be left out of some things without killing their force and effect—"The gates of hell shall not prevail," "They shall not pass."

Its overuse in England was demonstrated by a line in a play now in London called *Flowering Cherry,* in which a woman says, "I shall want to talk it over with my husband." Oh, she shall, will she? You either want to talk it over with your husband, or you don't, and you know it at the time.

15. I don't want to be the only one around here that (Let's not make that who, shall we?) keeps waking up and evoking the image of Ross getting snarled up in this sentence from [William Ernest] Henley: "One or two women (God bless them!) have loved me."

One or two women (God bless her or them!) has or have loved me.

"One or two" is another spelling of the word "several." Some of this may be in Fowler, I don't know. Some of it is a reasonable crapsimile of Fowler. For a long time now I have had a four-cornered exchange of letters—one of the others is Lewis Gannett—about this line, "The boy stood on the burning deck whence all but he had fled." Fowler and Gannett are for "he," whereas my position is that the boy was a goddamn fool not to get off that burning deck.

16. I have written three parodies of Henry James—I guess one of them is a what-you-call-it not triptych but that other thing, called "The Beast in the Dingle." It took me nine months to write and when Ross found this out he demanded to see it even though I had promised it to Cyril Connolly for his late lamented *Horizon.* This is the piece Ross gave back to me, saying, "I only understand 15 per cent of its illusions." I went back over the piece and I felt confident that he only understood 4 per cent of the illusions. That piece could have been printed in *The New Yorker* today, even though it's a darling of professors of English literature throughout mummum land. All of them know that I once intended to call it "The Return of the Screw."

17. Authors should sometimes consult editors about titles they want to use for their books ([William] Maxwell discussed *A Folded Leaf* with a lot of guys before he decided on it). In one year Gibbs and White and I came out with the world's most unwieldy titles, in order: "Bed of Neuroses," "Quo Vadimus? or The Case for the Bicycle," "The Middle-Aged Man on the Flying Trapeze." Incidentally, a woman in London asked me who had written "The Case for the Bisexual."

All pieces should be called by the best of *New Yorker* titles, "The Girls in Their Summer Dresses."

18. The what-you-call-it is a pastiche.

19. Editors should say to themselves, "Am I causative or costive or do I have a cause?" They should, I think, become trend fighters. "The Wings of the Falcon," combining two separate kinds of writing, could have gone in either of two different directions—the long, serious, comprehensive essay, or the short parody. It's true that the long essay was better done, but it is also true that the short parody could have been taken out, rewritten, and improved. The decline of humor in *The New Yorker* reflects the decline of humor in the world, in the country, and in the century. The unconscious trend is to encourage this decline, on behalf, God save us all, of "importance." The editorial board of every magazine should contain a practicing humorist. All our editors have humor but we have no practicing humorist and the belief has always been that such a person's opinion, as Ross used to say, was "without practical value."

I have never written more than a dozen pieces that I thought could not have been improved. Most writers who are any good have this belief about their work. Henry James made the mistake of rewriting some of his pieces, such as "The Reverberator," in his later years. But [F. O.] Matthiessen has painstakingly showed how this rewrite benefitted other stories and some of the novels. Editors, on the other hand, are inclined to arrive at rigidity of opinion. This is their greatest danger. Why don't you all get together and collaborate on "The Theory and Practice of Criticizing the Criticism of the Editing of *New Yorker* Articles"?

20. The Ross book by actual quote from Ross shows the development of one phase of *New Yorker* lunacy. The almost abject fear of repetitions, such opinion sheet lines as this, for example: "You have the word 'make' on galleys 3, 9, and 11." For God's sake.

Shakespeare used "to be" twice in one line and "tomorrow" three times in one line. Where were *The New Yorker* editors then? A curious flatness of style can occur where there are no repetitions, for repetitions are often the heart and spirit of poetic prose, and he who cannot write poetic prose is not a writer. Ross used to say we need a staff psychiatrist for the behavior of writers, but we need a staff psychologist for the understanding of the cyclical in the abilities and output of writers as well as for the seasonal ups and downs of individual editorial perception and ability. There are days when no surgeon should be allowed to operate. The biggest mistake I made here is when I insanely agreed to let somebody else try to cut out 4,500 words from a story of mine that was not intended for this magazine. If it were not for our lunacy we would all have known that was lunacy.

21. This magazine has had talk meetings, art meetings and news meetings, and at least one gathering of writers, to discuss the *Reader's Digest* crisis of some years ago. What it has never had, and badly needs, is a semi-annual meeting of Writers and Editors for the purpose of discussing the suggestions I have covered here, and others.

22. When Lobrano was alive he was one of two editors on the board of directors, but his place was taken by a corporation lawyer as *The New Yorker* moved slowly and inexorably from magazine to corporation. Lobrano should have been replaced by a writer or editor, unless, of course, our rivals and competitors are no longer magazines, but corporations. Does the danger lie in the increasing popularity of *Esquire* or in the fact that the American Can Company may drive us out of business?

23. There seems to have been a great, but groundless, fear that *The Years with Ross* would consist in part of an "attack" on *The New Yorker.* One learns how to take this kind of thing in his stride if he works here long enough, and I have been here 32 years this month. *The New Yorker* was born and brought up in the tradition of the spoiled child of literature. Hence it has always been able to dish it out and never able to take it. It took apart Luce and his magazines, to name just one man and organization it has taken apart, but it was scared to death that *Newsweek* would "attack" *The New Yorker.* I never saw so much panic in my life. The *Newsweek* article turned out to be a great big valentine. For a time, to avoid publicity, *New Yorker* editors actually seemed to believe that they could become anonymous. But no man can deny, or delegate, identity. Our hypersensitivity is perhaps our greatest fault. The tendency of such a tempera-

ment is to get both writers and editors down and to confuse the outside world. I move through all of this serenely, with occasional outbursts of rage or indignation, recently described by White as "explosions in the air high above 44th Street." If these explosions ever cease, it will be because I no longer love *The New Yorker* and I doubt that that could ever be possible.

In a letter to Frank Sullivan, Ross wrote, in his last year, "Thurber talks a lot about maturity."

I hadn't said maturity, I had said maturing, for I believe with Margaret Mead that maturity should be a goal never quite reached but always sought after. The process of going there is the process of human development.

JAMES THURBER

Unfamiliar Misquotations

It began in the country one Sunday morning at dawn when I was awakened by a phoebe. Without my glasses I could just see the light outside my windows, pallid, like the bust of Pallas, by no means rosy-fingered. The dawn of a new day, I thought drowsily . . . the dawn of a new world . . . the dawn of the World of Tomorrow . . . *the World of Tomorrow is too much with us.* I wanted to get up and write down that paraphrase of Wordsworth, which the mystery of association had brought to me. You know how it is when your mind stands with reluctant feet where the night and morning meet: an urgent perfection appears to shape your thoughts; the stream of consciousness runs so pure and clear you seem to see the pebbles of Truth on the bottom. Of course, after I had got up and lighted a cigarette and walked around, I realized that "The World of Tomorrow is too much with us" was really nothing to telephone the papers about, certainly not the New York papers. "What do you mean, 'too much'?" they would have asked. "What do you mean, 'us'?" "Me and Wordsworth," I would have answered, and they would have hung up. I got back in bed.

Since I couldn't go to sleep again, I took to recalling other old verses, and old maxims, which contained the word "world" or the word "tomorrow," and I began tinkering with them. None that I could remember seemed very apt; that's the trouble with becoming fully awake: a glory passes. "All the World of Tomorrow's a stage" gave me only a vague sense of satisfaction; "The World of Tomorrow, the flesh, and the devil" gave me none at all; I dismissed "The World of Tomorrow is my oyster" as both flippant and untrue. It couldn't be anybody's oyster. Certainly it is not mine. I suppose you should know right here that I am not fond of the World of Tomorrow, in capitals or in lower case, in Flushing or over the edges of time. No special reason; no hard feelings. I tried to think of some ancient line of poetry or of prose which would cast an amusing slur on these pleasure palaces in Xanadu. I thought I had it, finally, in "The World of Tomorrow and Tomorrow and Tomorrow creeps in this petty pace from day to day, to the last syllable of recorded time," but it occurred to me that it was too soon for that. That will be suitable for bitter chanting later on, when it begins to seem that this Fair will never end, that it must go on forever.

I realized, at a quarter of six, that I would have to go downstairs and get my Bartlett's *Familiar Quotations*; which I did, falling down the last four steps. The Bartlett's I own belonged to old Grandpa Taylor (whose father once killed a man with the flat of his hand) and it is the 1882 edition. This edition, according to a prefatory note, contains one hundred and twenty-five authors who were not represented in the edition of 1875. That seemed a frightful number of new authors to deal with before breakfast, but it came to me that if a hundred and twenty-five new authors have been added every seven years since 1882, the current Bartlett must contain a thousand writers who were not represented in my edition. I suddenly felt cozy with that old edition, chummy with Milton, almost a little lonely, there in the waxing light. I found that there were dozens of old writers who had made pronouncements about the world of their day which could easily be turned into pronouncements about the World of Tomorrow. If most of them are sad and some of them are savage, so run the worlds away.

Byron, of course (you will have remembered it), wrote the perfect line for those unhappy people living near the Fair who have lost such peace and quiet as they once had: "There's not a joy the World of Tomorrow can give like that it takes away." For those who want to dismiss the whole business lightly and have done with it, there is Francis Bacon's "The World of Tomorrow's a bubble," and Thomas Moore's "The World of Tomorrow is all a fleeting show." Horace Walpole goes into the thing more deeply: "The World of Tomorrow is a comedy to those who think, a tragedy to those who feel." A. F. F. von Kotzebue (1761–1819) has a slogan which he could sell

JAMES THURBER

to the San Francisco Exposition: "There is another and better World of Tomorrow." George Herbert believes you should get your mind on higher things and the hell with it: "Do well and right, and let the World of Tomorrow sink." Shakespeare comes out flatly against the gorgeous spectacle without making a single bone about it: "Vain pomp and glory of this World of Tomorrow, I hate ye." In case Mr. Whalen has convinced himself that all is well and everything is going to be all right, let him list to the Old Testament, which saith, "Boast not thyself of the World of Tomorrow; for thou knowest not what a day may bring forth." Good old Dryden has made his peace and had his fun and calmly awaits whatever may come: "World of Tomorrow, do thy worst, for I have lived today." And finally, Cowper sums up the general inadequacy of the whole enterprise in a quatrain:

What peaceful hours I once enjoy'd!
How sweet their memory still!
But they have left an aching void
The World of Tomorrow can never fill.

There must be hundreds of others in the latest Bartlett, and you can look them up yourself if you have a mind to. For those who don't care to confine themselves to verses or sayings which have the word "world" or "tomorrow" in them, on the ground that these could finally get to be a little stuffy, there is after all the whole field of proverbs and the whole range of paraphrasis. Just change any word or any phrase to read "World of Tomorrow." I'll show you what I mean; I'll start you off: "Who steals the World of Tomorrow steals trash." Lots of people, oh, millions, oh, hundreds of millions, will want to make up proverbs that glow and sparkle with a proper praise, and that is all right with me. I happen not to have been sleeping well and it makes me cross.

"It's nothing serious, Madam. They're writers."

JAMES THURBER

8 Important Characters in James Thurber's New Column.

If You Ask Me

(THE ENVELOPE OF MISCELLANY)

(James Thurber, who for years [and years] has been writing
what he feels, has turned to saying what he thinks for *PM*. His
brand new column, "If You Ask Me," will appear every Tuesday and Thursday, complete with opinion, guesswork, men,
women, dogs and seals. *[signed]* James Thurber)

Just the other afternoon I was going through an old Manila envelope
containing the odds and ends, the snippets and symbols of my life in
the 30s—the century's 30s and my own.

In the old envelope I found familiar and forgotten things: page
3 of a piece of mysterious writing, fluttering yellowly between a
vanished beginning and a lost ending, making no more sense than the
shouting of children at play on a frosty night; a dance program, a
challenge to a duel, a memorandum of heavy losses at the gaming
tables in Key West, a news item about an aged Columbus woman who
shot a truant officer ("I just pulled the trigger and let 'er go"), and,
in between everything, still as fresh and sharp and clear as ever, a
timely anecdote sent in to *The New Yorker* by a man named Price in
1931.

Attached to this long buried message from the past was a slip of
red paper meaning: "Rush! Priority A!" On the red slip was written
in only slightly faded pencil: "Must go this week." Nothing had ever
been done about it.

My executors, in their stiff collars and Sunday shoes, will come
upon it in a mysterious safety-deposit box containing, in addition to

the urgent anecdote, a box of carbide for old-fashioned motorcycle lamps, three blank checks signed by Button Gwinnett (signature forged), and a telegram (undelivered) to Rush Holt.

I will have to have a separate old Manila envelope for letters like the two that arrived last week under the same cover. This cover also contained three or four poems in longhand. One of the two letters in this remarkable envelope (on which was printed "The Woman") was from an old cook of mine in Connecticut named Martha; the other letter was from Louise Denny, who is associated with a magazine called *Modern Woman,* to Helen Stelzenmuller, assistant editor of *The Woman;* the poems were by my former cook's sister Dorothea, who Martha tells me lives in Hoboken, N.J., and is gifted.

You may wonder why Martha's introduction of her sister and her sister's work should be all tangled up with an exchange of professional amenities between Miss Denny and Miss Stelzenmuller. However, it finally turned out Martha decided that the simplest way to reach me would be by writing to a magazine called *The Man.*

The editor of *The Man* (an impatient and suspicious fellow named Quackenbush) turned the letter over to Miss Stelzenmuller, editor of *The Woman.* Miss Stelzenmuller, who is not so impatient as Mr. Quackenbush, but even more suspicious, hastily stuffed Martha's letter, Dorothea's poems, and Miss Denny's letter into an envelope and sent them all on to me.

Not a man who is easily outdone, I am sending Miss Stelzenmuller an envelope containing three drawings of Fort Sumter by my young niece, a copy of *Out Where the West Begins,* and a letter from a California woman to her daughter at college, advising her to have her teeth out if they (the teeth) are pushing her teeth out.

This letter from the California woman, found on a Hollywood street by Mr. Richard Connell, was sent on to me by Mr. Connell, probably in the hope that I would not know what to do with it. As for Dorothea's poems and the letter from Miss Denny to Miss Stelzenmuller, I have put them in a plain white envelope and sent them off to Mr. Connell. Give him something to think about.

The Book-End

THURBER ON OTHER WRITERS

Excerpts from
"The Book-End," 1923

They have started selecting the ten books to take to a desert island with one again. The *International Book Review* has had some notable writers select their ten; a newspaper syndicate publishes the selections of prominent people, and other publications have caught the spirit of the thing. We thought this indoor sport died out about eight years ago when James Mongomery Flagg went to the head of the class by picking nine books of cigaret papers and old Irv' Cobb's *Back Home.*

Why not select the ten movie actresses whom you would prefer to take to a desert island? Ourself, we select nine copies of Norma Talmadge, and Pauline Garon.

* * *

To die as Jim Faulkner died is not death at all. It is merely ceasing to be, tangibly, in the places where one has been. And tangibility is an unsatisfactory thing, and of all things the most transitory. Some of us have little more than that. We impinge on the consciousness of our fellow beings and when the stimulus is gone there is nothing left but the memory of an image, and that is death. But those rare souls whose spirit gets magically into the hearts of men, leave behind them something more real and warmly personal than bodily presence, an ineffable and eternal thing. It is everlasting life touching us as something more than a vague, recondite concept. The sound of a great name dies like an echo; the splendor of fame fades into nothing; but the grace of a fine spirit pervades forever the places through which it has passed, like the haunting loveliness of mignonette in the O. Henry story. It is the surest intimation that we may have of immortality. Such was the spirit of James W. Faulkner.

* * *

Anyone who reads at all diversely during these bizarre nineteen twenties cannot escape the conclusion that a number of crazy men and women are writing stuff which remarkably passes for important composition among certain persons who should know better. Mr. Stuart P. Sherman, however, refused to be numbered among those who stand in awe and admiration of one of the most eminent of the idiots, Gertrude Stein. He reviews her *Geography and Plays* in the Aug. 11 issue of the *Literary Review* of the *New York Evening Post* and arrives at the conviction that it is a marvellous and painstaking achievement in setting down approximately 80,000 words which mean nothing at all.

Mr. Sherwood Anderson, who, in the course of some worthwhile writings has got off huge sections of imbecilic vagaries, whoops it up every now and then for Gertrude and has written in that vein an introduction to her barrel of words. Just one of several quotations from Miss Stein is enough upon which to rest one's case: "When she was quite a young one she knew she had been in a family living and that that family living was one that anyone could be one not have been having if they were to be one being one not thinking about being one having been having family living." That, it appears, is part of a "Portrait of Constance Fletcher."

Some months ago we resolved to enter wholeheartedly into the movement to embrace the obscurely amazing as the genuinely important and strove to sustain the belief that Ben Hecht's *Erik Dorn,* for example, is hot intellectual stuff. But the strain upon our natural tastes, sophomoric and old-fashioned as they may be, was too great. We return to James and Hergesheimer and Conrad, to beautiful words so arranged as to present truthful ideas intelligibly. In Hecht and Stein, the poetry of Amy Lowell at its oddest, the works of James Joyce and Anderson and T. S. Eliot may be the beginnings of a modern literature which shall eventually obliterate the memory of the old order of sentences and sense; but we trust that such legal

JAMES THURBER

prohibition of the old stuff as may eventually be written into the law of the land will not carry with it a penalty for possession in one's home of the books one has learned, in his unenlightened way, to love.

* * *

Mr. Charles Norris has added *Bread* to his list of monosyllabic novels, of which the first two were *Salt* and *Brass.* We rapidly lose interest in any writer who is so easily entertained, or who, by some unaccountable back alley of reasoning, comes to the conclusion that it is striking to name his books in that manner. *Salt* was, in some ways and in some chapters, a fine piece of work. It drew, for one thing, the most authentic picture of what was called in that day "chicken" that has ever been drawn. But it had too much moralizing and this-is-the-waying, and alas-alasing in it, and it actually ended up with a paragraph saying, in effect, here let us leave them, confident that they will get along all right from now on, etc.

This business of naming novels after food and plumbing is but one step removed from the peculiar desideratum of Louis Joseph Vance, who some years ago swore or bet or something he could write ten or twelve books, the titles of which should each have two words beginning with "B"—the *Brass Bowl, Bronze Bell, Black Bag,* etc.—we forget how many he actually did before the fever wore off or the keeper came to tell him his army was waiting.

The movies just love to jump upon such novels, however, tie-and-dye them, place rosettes in their buttonholes, stand a huge ormolu clock on their mantel, plaster a rococo cornice on their eaves, and, turning to the admiring people, exclaim, "Voila!—a super-extra-de luxe photoplay!" "Is Your Wedding Ring Brass?" was the batik wall hanging they finally made out of *Brass.* "Does Your Bread Weigh a Pound?" will probably be the companion piece they will weave out of the newest novel.

* * *

Idle Thought of a Busy Literatus.
    One great advantage which poetry has over prose—one sense in

which, we might even say, it is considerably more beautiful—is that it fills up space approximately three times as rapidly.

* * *

Among the books we have been trying to get around to, without any success so far, are *Jacob's Room,* by Virginia Woolf; *The Dancer in the Shrine,* by Amanda Benjamin Hall; *The Flower in Drama,* by Stark Young; *A Pocketful of Poses,* by Anne Parrish (we like a picture we saw of her recently); *Fiery Particles,* by C. E. Montague; and *The Judge,* by Rebecca West.

Add things which mean nothing in my life: the autographed edition of the words of Mr. James Oliver Curwood.

Among the books which we don't intend to get around to are *Structural Steelwork,* by William H. Black; *Pung Chow: The Game of a Hundred Intelligences,* New York: Schilling; *Annual Report of the Bureau of American Ethnology; Black Oxen,* by Gertrude Atherton; *Ten Nights in a Radio Head-set,* by Alton D. Spencer; *Gargoyles,* by Ben Hecht; and *The Dynamo, Its Theory, Design and Manufacture,* by C. C. Hawkins.

Among the books which we really ought to get around to, we suppose, is *Tobacco and Mental Efficiency,* by M. V. O'Shea.

* * *

The award of the Pulitzer Prize for 1922 to Willa Cather's *One of Ours,* favorably mentioned by this department last week, has aroused protests from many critics who loudly assert that *Babbitt* was the best American novel of last year. It was. But the award was not made for the best novel, in the sense in which Heywood Broun and the rest of the Algonquins mean it, but for the book which "best presents the wholesome atmosphere of American life and the highest standard of American manners and manhood." Mr. Sinclair Lewis does not deal with the wholesome atmosphere of American life or the highest standard of American manners and manhood. He deals with 100 per cent Americanism.

Narrowed as the field is by the requirements fixed by the committee, few meritorious novels of the nineteen-twenties can fall within it. The thing we rejoice in is that the award went to Miss Cather and not to Zane Grey or Gene Stratton Porter. The author of *My Ántonia* is one of the few important novelists in this country who do not confine themselves altogether to realistic portrayals of the lives of Klux kleagles, morons, defectives, psychopaths, sex-starvelings, wealthy realtors, plate glass manufacturers who covet widows, small town garage proprietors who covet the wives of the hotel managers, and miscellaneous wives and widows and other women with grotesquely improper desiderata.

* * *

This Testimonial, Carl, Has All the Contour of a Tongue in the Cheek.

(We lift it from the jacket of Stratford Publishing Co. books.)

A tribute from Carl Sandburg, one of the prize winners for the two best books of poems published in 1918—

Dear Dr. Schnittkind:

I like the whole general drift of your books—you look to me like a builder.

Now we know of one other publisher who looks to us like a third-baseman, but after all, personal appearance is no reliable criterion. However, as Herman Miller wrote us, apropos of the Sandburg tribute, "If we are to be builders, we must deal more and more with the concrete."

"Am I the only woman in America who isn't writing novels?"

JAMES THURBER

More Authors Cover
the Snyder Trial

I
WHO DID WE DID DID WE WE DID, SAYS MISS STEIN!
By Gertrude Stein

This is a trial. This is quite a trial. I am on trial. They are on trial. Who is on trial?

I can tell you how it is. I can tell you have told you will tell you how it is.

There is a man. There is a woman. There is not a man. There would have been a man. There was a man. There were two men. There is one man. There is a woman where is a woman is a man.

He says he did. He says he did not. She says she did. She says she did not. She says he did. He says she did. She says they did. He says they did. He says they did not. She says they did not. I'll say they did.

II
JOYCE FINDS SOCKSOCKING IS BIG ELEMENT
IN MURDER CASE!
By James Joyce

Trial regen by trialholden Queenscountycourthouse with tumpetty taptap mid socksocking with sashweights by jackals. In socksocking, the sashwiring goes: guggengaggleoggogsnukkkk. . . . To corsetsale is to alibi is to meetinlovenkillenlove. *Rehab des arbah sed drahab!* Not a quart of papa's booze had poison booze vor the killparty for the snugglesnuggle. . . .

III
OUT A MILE, WRITES COBB!
By Ty Cobb

Stealing home from a bridge game is a clever stunt, if properly worked. But it should never be followed by the hit-and-run play.

It's not like the Cry Baby bandits—four bawls and a walk to Sing Sing. Snyder merely hit into a double play and was out a mile, Syracuse to New York to Syracuse.

JAMES THURBER

If You Ask Me

(THOMAS WOLFE)

"What novel in your memory has received such praise as this?" Harper's asks in an advertisement, referring to Thomas Wolfe's new book. The praise that is then set down as the highest within your recollection or mine reads like this: "One of the most vital and wide-embracing pictures of American life," "An authentic work of art, of genius," "Finest, most mature book he ever wrote," "He will stand with Melville," ". . . a tide mark."

Anybody who reads book reviews fairly consistently would reply, without hesitation, to Harper's question: "About 1,100 novels in my memory have received such praise as this."

A few years ago Mr. Geoffrey Hellman, in a searching examination of American book reviews, found a bushel-basketful of paeans of praise for novels, any one of which would make Harper's little collection look like unmitigated disapproval. John Cowper Powys, for his *Wolf Solent,* was compared not only to Melville but to Dickens, Hardy, Shakespeare, Dante, Keats, Shelley, Congreve, Whitman, and Carlyle. At least twice a month, as all readers of book reviews know, a new genius emerges and sets an all-time All-American tide mark with a vital and all-embracing picture of American life that is haunting and unforgettable and filled with a unique power and a strange and moving beauty.

I have never been able to read very far in Thomas Wolfe. I have asked, as Mr. Mencken used to do in such cases, for divine support but I am simply not strong enough to battle my way through Wolfe's thunderous tides and swim out to the "confused but intuitive sense of the apparent meaning and pattern of Life," which is said to lie somewhere in the vast surging ocean of his 735-page novels.

The critics will tell you that this is conventional criticism and that you should not look for Form where there is Divine Fire. I restrain the impulse to reply to this, quite simply, "Nuts!" It seems to me the conventional excuse advanced on behalf of the Genius. He is not supposed to labor over an idea until he cuts it down from 6,700 sprawling words to the three paragraphs which will express it perfectly, that is, bring it within the definition of Art. The critics not only excused the big good Wolfe's sprawl, but convinced themselves and him that his mystic talents demanded the sprawl, and so he sprawled more and more as *Time and the River* rolled on from novel to novel.

If Thomas Wolfe had lived, it seems likely that his literary house would have become more and more littered and dusty. He did not believe in winding the clocks or cleaning the silver; he never swept the floor or washed the window panes; long, untrimmed essays grew up in the window boxes of his prose and were not plucked out. That kind of housekeeping may be Divine Fire but it isn't art.

Author's note: *Defenses of Mr. Wolfe and attacks on this column must be double-spaced on a typewriter equipped with a fresh black ribbon.*

*"This is my house, Mr. Wolfe, and
if you don't get out I'll throw you out!"*

COLLECTING HIMSELF

"He looks a little like Thomas Wolfe, and he certainly makes the most of it."

Recommended Reading

West Cornwall, Conn.
May 15, 1949

Dear Miss Whitaker:

. . . One of my closest friends, a former professor of English, who was one of the best amateur actors I have ever known, deplored, just before his death last month, the fact that Rosie is going to attend a college given over entirely to the teaching of dramatics. He felt that the best actors and actresses were the product of life and literature, rather than of merely technical study. I have had this in mind also, and one of my graduation presents to Rosie is a list of some 20 books, most of them under 90,000 words, all of them beautifully written, which I thought might help to supply the lack of a general arts course in college. I have felt that she could write as well as act, but she seems to believe that writing is "too hard." This is definite proof that she knows about writing. I will let the future take care of her career. It is foolish for a father to worry about his daughter, and even more foolish to worry about her career. If he expects a scrapbook full of favorable reviews of her acting or her writing, he is likely to get instead a couple of granddaughters—this makes him a much luckier man. . . .

Sincerely yours,

JAMES THURBER

EDITOR'S NOTE: James and Althea's daughter, Rosemary, attended Northampton School for Girls. Sarah B. Whitaker, headmistress, received these letters from Thurber.

West Cornwall, Conn.
June 1, 1949

Dear Miss Whitaker:

. . . Since Rosie is intent on the theater, I have decided to let her keep
that difficult dream until it comes true or she finds out she doesn't
want it. I have felt that she could become a writer, but years ago she
said it was too hard. I am on the soundest ground of experience when
I say that for every one young male writer who gives up I have found
a half dozen girls in New York who could not stand rewriting or
rejections. I think that 17 is too young for her to know what she wants
to do or actually can do, and since this is true, all decisions are hard
to make.

   The list of books I am giving her consists largely of short novels
that interested, inspired, or excited me for their story, their style,
their originality, or some other quality. They are all easy to read and
calculated to prove that worthwhile writing, by Americans and English in this century, can be as absorbing as novels like *Centennial
Summer* which Rosie read largely because of the movie. I have long
contemplated an article for *Harper's* on the problem of literature for
the young. I was a great reader from the time I was 10, but most
of my enthusiasms in high school and college I found outside class.
I am a rabid antagonist of the *Silas Marner* kind of required reading.
Neither this nor *The Spy,* nor *The Talisman,* nor *The Return of the
Native* stirred my interest as a writer and appreciator as much as the
good books I read for myself. I realize that the question of content,
especially the sexual, is difficult for teachers everywhere in the case
of the adolescent. Rosie, however, will soon be 18, at which [age]
my grandmother had two children, and I think that she will discover
in reading these books that writing can be fun. In preparation for my
article, on which I have much research to do, I have discovered,
neither to my dismay nor surprise, that most school girls of 17 have
read the sexy parts of *God's Little Acre* and *Appointment in Samarra,* to
mention two. They get it out of context and in distortion, exchanging
books in which pages are marked, never beginning or ending the
books. I was disappointed to see that such a lovely thing as *My Ántonia*
could become uninteresting to Rosie in prospect merely because it
was listed in a reading list. I expect the young girl would come to hate
that heroine, but I hope that *A Lost Lady* and *My Mortal Enemy* will

restore her belief in Willa Cather. I do not believe they would affect her faith in the American woman, and if she has the creative talent I suspect, she will get more out of the story and the style than she will out of its fictional facts.

This is not, needless to say, my selection of the Great Books; it is merely intended as a stimulation to a young lady, who if she ever reads them, may happily discover that writing may be hard, but also desirable, and as exciting as the theater. I will send her other books as she grows older. There are many she had read, including E. B. White's *One Man's Meat,* whose perfect writing should be on every reading list.

Many of these books I have not read for 15 years or longer, but in thinking about short books that affected me as a writer, I arrived at this selection. There are dexterity here, flexibility, color, humor, suspense, and a variety of moods, and a full course in plot and construction. You will note that the women writers are well represented. . . .

I look forward to seeing you at graduation.

Cordially yours,

JAMES THURBER

Babbitt, Sinclair Lewis
Daisy Miller, Henry James
Gentle Julia, Booth Tarkington
Linda Condon, Java Head, Wild Oranges, Joseph Hergesheimer
The Wanderer, Alain-Fournier
The Great Gatsby, F. Scott Fitzgerald
The Sun Also Rises, Ernest Hemingway
Invitation to the Waltz, Rosamond Lehmann
This Simian World, God and My Father, Clarence Day
The House in Paris, Elizabeth Bowen
A Lost Lady, My Mortal Enemy, Willa Cather
A Handful of Dust, Decline and Fall, Evelyn Waugh
Heaven's My Destination, The Cabala, Thornton Wilder
February Hill, The Wind at My Back, Victoria Lincoln

Blue Voyage, Conrad Aiken
The Bitter Tea of General Yen, G. Z. Stone
Lady into Fox, Edward Garnett
How to Write Short Stories, Ring Lardner
The Return of the Soldier, Rebecca West
Miss Lonelyhearts, Nathanael West

. . . Last June I sent twenty-four books to my seventeen-year-old daughter, on her graduation from the Northampton School for Girls. Each of them had excited me at one period or another during the past thirty years. All of them are comparatively short, and most of them are out of print. Some of them I have reread more than once, but others I have never had time or chance to get back to. It had taken several months to round them all up. . . .

What I hoped this shelf would prove is that reading can be fun, that modern writing can be good, and that good writing can be exciting. The adolescent who is plunged into *Ivanhoe, Silas Marner,* and *Great Expectations* is likely to believe that respectable writing must be old and mossy, and that respectable writers died in the eighteenth or nineteenth century. If he is a child of any creative talent, he may turn to one of the livelier arts—the theatre, or music, or painting, or ballet dancing. Maybe this is what has become of our young writers. Of all my two dozen books, I have found only *My Ántonia* on any of the school reading lists I have seen, but *The Robe* appears on a lot of them.

No two persons, of course, would pick the same twenty-four books to give to anyone, and if I were to compile my list again, I would probably throw several out and put some others in. My system, at the time, was simply to sit and remember the short books I'd read, and when one of them struck the bell in my memory, I wrote its title down. We all have our literary idiosyncrasies and blind spots. H. L. Mencken used to pray to God for guidance, so that he might be made to see what merit there was in the works of D. H. Lawrence. For some reason, or possibly out of pure cussedness, I have never been able to get very far in Norman Douglas's *South Wind,* and although I am a great Max Beerbohm man, *Zuleika Dobson* leaves me cold. I left out *The Red Badge of Courage* because death in battle isn't for girls, and *Serena Blandish* because a lady of impeccable literary taste told me that the day I liked Serena must have been one of my bad days. This same

critic read *Wild Oranges* before I shipped it off and told me that it is
pretty terrible—seems to be full of expressions like "said the former"
and "replied the latter." Well, it has been nearly thirty years since I
read this one. *The Bridge of San Luis Rey* never fetched me, and I
couldn't make up my mind about Sylvia Warner's *Mr. Fortune's Maggot.* A little old item called *The Inn of the Silver Moon,* by one Knicker-
bocker Viele, if my memory serves, either delighted me in 1914 or
appalled me, I can't remember which. I omitted from my collection
Appointment in Samarra and *God's Little Acre,* not because they are too
"sexy," to use a lady teacher's word, but because I was reliably
informed that all seventeen-year-old girls have read them secretly.

Secondary schools must proceed primly on the rule and theory
that books intimating or revealing the facts of life shall be taboo. The
truth is, of course, that this merely adds incentive to the eager exploration of family and public library shelves, and the trouble with the
system of taboo is that only the dubious pages are read by a youngster
when he comes upon the treasure of a banned book. I am much too
old and tired to attempt to solve this problem now. Besides, there is
a wasp in the room. . . .

What Price Conquest?

There is, I regret to say, a kind of lamplight playing over the mood and style, the events and figures, of Mr. Steinbeck's new short novel about the people of a small conquered town and its conquerors. I suspect that if a writer conceives of a war story in terms of a title like *The Moon Is Down* he is likely to get himself into soft and dreamy trouble. Maybe a title like *Guts in the Mud* would have produced a more convincing reality. Anyway, this little book needs more guts and less moon. An impatient friend of mine who had read it, too, said to me, "It is probably Robert Nathan's best book." Whomever you may be reminded of, the vastly talented Mr. Steinbeck has definitely taken on here a new phrase and a new temper. One wonders what kind of thing he will do next.

The reader of this book does not have to be told that the author had a stage version in mind as he wrote it (the play has gone into rehearsal as I set this down). This has had the unfortunate effect of giving the interiors in the novel the feel of sets. I could not believe that the people who enter Mayor Orden's living room come from the streets and houses of a little town. They come from their dressing rooms. The characters and the language they speak are in keeping with the theatrical atmosphere, from Annie, the irate cook, to Colonel Lanser, the leader of the invaders, and his staff. If these are German officers, if they are anything else but American actors, I will eat the manuscript of your next play.

The point upon which Mr. Steinbeck in these pages has so lovingly and gently brooded is that there are no machines and no armies mighty enough to conquer the people. "The people don't like to be conquered, sir," says Mayor Orden to Colonel Lanser, "and so they will not be." This shining theme is restated a great many times, principally by one of the invading officers whose nerves have been worn down by the cold eyes and the silent faces of the little people of the little town. Lieutenant Tonder in *The Moon Is Down* goes to pieces and raves, and this scene demands comparison with the going-to-pieces scene of Lieutenant Moore in *What Price Glory?* and that of Lieutenant Hibbert in *Journey's End*. Apparently Laurence Stallings and Maxwell Anderson, who did the scene first (and best) have contributed a convention to the war play of our time. I can only say after reading the three scenes at one sitting that if the German lieutenants of today are really like Lieutenant Tonder, then the American Moores and the British Hibberts will be able to rout the pussycats merely by shouting "Boo!"

Let us listen to Lieutenant Tonder in *The Moon Is Down:*

"I want a girl. I want to go home. I want a girl. There's a girl in this town, a pretty girl. I see her all the time. She has blond hair. She lives beside the old-iron store. I want that girl. . . .

"That's it! The enemy's everywhere! Every man, every woman, even children! The enemy's everywhere! Their faces look out of doorways. The white faces behind the curtains, listening. We have beaten them, we have won everywhere, and they wait and obey, and they wait. Half the world is ours. . . .

"What do the reports say about us? Do they say we are cheered, loved, flowers in our paths? Oh, these horrible people waiting in the snow! . . .

"Conquered and we're afraid; conquered and we're surrounded. . . . I had a dream—or a thought—out in the snow with the black shadows and the faces in the doorways, the cold faces behind curtains. I had a thought or a dream. . . .

"Conquest after conquest, deeper and deeper into molasses. . . . Maybe the Leader is crazy. Flies conquer the flypaper. Flies capture two hundred miles of new flypaper!"

Now listen to Lieutenant Moore in *What Price Glory?:*

"Oh, God, Dave, but they got you. God, but they got you a beauty, the dirty swine. God DAMN them for keeping us up here in this hellish town. Why can't they send in some of the million men they've got back there and give us a chance? Men in my platoon are so hysterical every time I get a message from Flagg, they want to know if they're being relieved. What can I tell them? They look at me like whipped dogs—as if I had just beaten them—and I've had enough of them this time. I've got to get them out, I tell you. They've had enough. Every night the same way. (He turns to Flagg.) And since six o'clock there's been a wounded sniper in the tree by that orchard angle crying *'Kamerad! Kamerad!'* Just like a big crippled whippoorwill. What price glory now? Why in God's name can't we all go home? Who gives a damn for this lousy, stinking little town but the poor French bastards who live here? God damn it! You talk about courage, and all night long you hear a man who's bleeding to death on a tree calling you *'Kamerad'* and asking you to save him. God damn every son of a bitch in the world who isn't here! I won't stand for it. I won't stand for it! I won't have the platoon asking me every minute of the livelong night when they are going to be relieved. . . . Flagg, I tell you you can shoot me, but I won't stand for it. . . . I'll take 'em out tonight and kill you if you get in my way. . . ."

At one point in *The Moon Is Down* the little people of the town are aided by the falling of a curious manna from Heaven: small blue parachutes come drifting to earth, carrying dynamite and chocolate. The little children of the conquered town go hunting for the candy with as much excitement as if they were searching for Easter eggs. The Steinbeck story will make a very pretty movie.

I keep wondering what the people of Poland would make of it all.

* * *

EDITOR'S NOTE: In a subsequent issue of *The New Republic* (March 30, 1942), Thurber replied to Mr. Marshall A. Best, who felt that Thurber's review was "a slap in the face" and expressed that "softy cynicism that might yet lose us the war." Rather than the "more guts and less moon" that Thurber recommended, Mr. Best urged "more dynamite and chocolate, and fewer owls in the attic!"

JAMES THURBER

Sir: Mr. Best will not have to look far to see that the question of what the people of Poland would think of *The Moon Is Down* has been brought out of the subjunctive and into the present indicative. He will live, I think, to see many more letters protesting against Mr. Steinbeck's gentle fable of War in Wonderland, not only from Poles who have endured German conquest, but from Jugoslavs, Greeks, French, Dutch, and all the rest. Mr. Best is quite right when he says that we might yet lose the war. Nothing would help more toward that end than for Americans to believe Steinbeck's version of Nazi conquest instead of its true story of hell, horror, and hopelessness. This true story may be found, to name just one place, on page 10 of the *New York Times* for March 19, in a summary of a Polish White Book dealing with the German conquest of Poland. The mass rape and systematic debauchery of the women of a conquered country stand in curious contrast to Mr. Steinbeck's idyllic picture of a lonely German officer who simply wants to talk and hold hands with the widow of a man the Nazis have murdered. I should like to send a clipping of this to Mr. Marshall A. Best, Managing Editor, The Viking Press (publishers of *The Moon Is Down*), by whose fuzzy mental distress and public heartbreak I am approximately as deeply moved as I would be by the tears of a real-estate agent.

I am sorry about that slap in the face. I didn't realize my hand was open.

"I told Womrath's I don't want to read anything instructive until the war ends."

JAMES THURBER

"Your faith is really more disturbing than my atheism."

"*Professor Townsend is really too high-strung to be a philosopher.*"

JAMES THURBER

Taps at Assembly

The novel F. Scott Fitzgerald was working on when he died in December 1940 has been on the counters for three months now. His publishers tell me that it has sold only about 3,500 copies. This indicates, I think, that it has fallen, and will continue to fall, into the right hands. In its unfinished state, *The Last Tycoon* is for the writer, the critic, the sensitive appreciator of literature. The book, I have discovered, can be found in very few Womrath stores or other lending libraries. This, one feels sure, would have pleased Scott Fitzgerald. The book would have fared badly in the minds and discussions of readers who read books simply to finish them.

Fitzgerald's work in progress was to have told the life story of a big Hollywood producer. In the form in which the author left it, it runs to six chapters, the last one unfinished. There follows a synopsis of what was to have come, and then there are twenty-eight pages of notes, comments, descriptive sentences and paragraphs, jotted down by the author, and a complete letter he wrote outlining his story idea. All these were carefully selected and arranged by Edmund Wilson (who also contributes a preface) and anyone interested in the ideas and craftsmanship of one of America's foremost fiction writers will find them exciting reading. Mr. Wilson has also included *The Great Gatsby* in the volume, and the five short stories which he considers likely to be of permanent interest. His choices are "The Rich Boy," "The Diamond as Big as the Ritz," "May Day," "Absolution," and "Crazy Sunday." This collection belongs on a shelf of every proud library.

No book published here in a long time has created more discussion and argument among writers and lovers of writing than *The Last Tycoon.* Had it been completed, would it have been Fitzgerald's best book? Should it, in a draft which surely represented only the middle stages of rewriting, have been published alongside the flawless final writing of *The Great Gatsby*? In the larger view, it is sentimental nonsense to argue against the book's publication. It was the last work of a first-rate novelist; it shows his development, it rounds out his all too brief career; it gives us what he had done and indicates what he was going to do on the largest canvas of his life; it is filled with a great many excellent things as it stands. It is good to be acquainted with all these things. In the smaller, the personal view, there is a valid argument, however. Writers who rewrite and rewrite until they reach the perfection they are after consider anything less than that perfection nothing at all. They would not, as a rule, show it to their wives or to their most valued friends. Fitzgerald's perfection of style and form, as in *The Great Gatsby,* has a way of making something that lies between your stomach and your heart quiver a little.

The Last Tycoon is the story of Monroe Stahr, one of the founders of Hollywood, the builder of a movie empire. We see him in his relation to the hundreds of human parts of the vast machine he has constructed, and in his relation to the woman he loves, and to a Communist Party organizer (their first contact is one of the best and most promising parts of the book). We were to have seen him on an even larger scale, ending in a tremendous upheaval and disintegration of his work and his world and a final tragedy. Fitzgerald would have brought it off brilliantly in the end. This would have been another book in the fine one-color mood of *The Great Gatsby,* with that book's sure form and sure direction. He had got away from what he calls the "deterioration novel" that he wrote in *Tender Is the Night.* He had a long way yet to go in *The Last Tycoon* and his notes show that he realized this.

In one of these notes he tells himself that his first chapter is "stilted from rewriting" and he instructs himself to rewrite it, not from the last draft, but from mood. It is good as it stands, but he knew it wasn't right. In the last of the notes, Fitzgerald had written, with all the letters in capitals: "ACTION IS CHARACTER." A brilliant perfectionist in the managing of his ultimate effects, Fitzgerald knew that Stahr had been too boldly blocked out in the draft which has come to us. There was too much direct description of the great man. He fails to live up to it all. Such a passage as this would surely have been done over: "He had flown up very high to see, on strong wings, when he was young. And while he was up there he had looked on all the kingdoms, with the kind of eyes that can stare straight into the sun. Beating his wings tenaciously—finally frantically—and keeping on beating them, he had stayed up there longer than most of us, and then, remembering all he had seen from his great height of how things were, he had settled gradually to earth." There are other large, unhewn lines which would have given place to something else, such as this speech by one of his worshipers: "So I came to you, Monroe. I never saw a situation where you didn't know a way out. I said to myself: even if he advises me to kill myself, I'll ask Monroe." The Monroe Stahr we see is not yet the man this speaker is talking about. I would like to see him as he would have emerged from one or two more rewrites of what is here, excellent, sharp, witty, and moving as a great deal of it is.

It must inevitably seem to some of us that Fitzgerald could not have set himself a harder task than that of whipping up a real and moving interest in Hollywood and its great and little men. Although the movie empire constitutes one of the hugest and therefore one of the most important industries in the world, it is a genuine feat, at least for me, to pull this appreciation of Bel-Air and Beverly Hills from the mind down into the emotions, where, for complete and satisfying surrender to a novel and its people, it properly belongs. It is a high tribute to Scott Fitzgerald to say that he would have accomplished this. I know of no one else who could.

Everyone will be glad to find "The Rich Boy" and "Absolution" included among the short stories in the volume. "Crazy Sunday" is perhaps of value to the student of Fitzgerald because it contains the germ of "The Last Tycoon," but I find it impossible to sustain a permanent, or even a passing, interest in the personalities and problems of the Hollywood persons it is concerned with. A lot of us will always be interested in "Babylon Revisited," even though it is the pet of the professors of English who compile anthologies; and I mourn the absence of "A Short Trip Home" whether you do or not.

If You Ask Me

(ANNE MORROW LINDBERGH)

The most disturbing book I have read in a long time is Anne Morrow Lindbergh's little confession of faith, *The Wave of the Future*. If you have already heard about it, it won't do any harm to hear about it again; anyway, I can't write about anything else at the moment.

Mrs. Lindbergh's prefiguring of what is to come gives me the creeblies; it sets the weeping wailwice scuttering along the edges of my dreams. She has no vision of a world of tomorrow in which Fascism has been overthrown. From her meditations, her travels, and her reading of Whitehead, she has constructed her own *mystique* of the course of history from now on. It goes something like this: out of Man's sins and mistakes, out of his greed, his Godlessness, and his pride of possession has come a Reaching for Light known variously

as Fascism, Nazism, and Communism. We must look beyond the
petty aims of conquest and destruction, beyond the mad and bloody
leaders, and discern a natural mutation in the story of people on this
planet. The "goodness" and the "necessity" at the heart of this mutation is the wave of the future; on the New Order, purged of its evils
and its atrocities, will be built the future life of mankind. To this clean
and perfect foundation France will contrive, God knows how, to
make her beautiful contribution and England, whether defeated or
not, hers.

Mrs. Lindbergh believes that in this war the "Forces of the Past"
are fighting the "Forces of the Future," a sorry and futile fight for the
Past. She hates to see the things she loved go, but they are dying. It
is perhaps because of this that she always put the word "democracies"
in quotation marks, and, once, the word "liberty." It gave me the
sickening feeling that, for her, these things as we have known them
are already dead and buried.

Mrs. Lindbergh does not refer to Nazism and its allied tyrannies
as "evil systems"; she uses such expressions as "the things we deplore
in these systems," "the things we dislike in Nazism." This is because
of her belief in the goodness of the Wave of the Future when what
she calls the "scum" has been cleared away from it.

"No one today defends the atrocities of the French Revolution,"
she says, "but few seriously question the fundamental necessity and
'rightness' of the movement." There is her parallel for what is going
on today, necessity, rightness, and all. This is not a difficult parallel
for a lady to draw who sees in her "Forces of the Future" "some new
conception of humanity and its place in the world."

Mrs. Lindbergh naturally wants us to stay out of a war which is
not a Crusade against Evil but merely a foolish battle against the
inexorable forces of History, Destiny, and the Future. What she
wants us to do she describes in a patriotic and poetic passage full of
allusions to the white churches of New England and so on. We must
bring about, by some kind of domestic revolution or reformation, a
spirit equal to the national spirit of Germany and the national spirit
of England under Churchill. How this spirit, which was created on
the one hand by a desire for vengeance and on the other by a necessity for defense, can be created in a country to which she leaves so

little for anyone to fight for or against, I have no idea. You can't start such a spirit by singing ballads or by thinking of Lincoln. You can't start one by reading Mrs. Lindbergh's sorrowful little book, or by listening to her husband.

The Odyssey *of Disney*

I have never particularly cared for the *Odyssey* of Homer. The edition we used in high school—I forget the editors' names, but let us call it Bwumba and Bwam's edition—was too small to hide a livelier book behind, and it was cold and gray in style and in content. All the amorous goings on of the story were judiciously left out. We pupils might, at that age, have taken a greater interest in T. E. Shaw's recent rendering, the twenty-eighth, by his count, in English; for bang-off in Book I the third sentence reads: "She craved him for her bed-mate: while he was longing for his house and wife." But there wasn't any such sentence in old Bwumba and Bwam. It was a pretty dull book to read. No matter how thin Mr. Shaw has sliced it, it is still, it seems to me, a pretty dull book to read.

The fact that the *Odyssey* is the "oldest book worth reading for its story and the first novel of modern Europe" makes it no more lively—to me, anyway—than does the turning of it into what Mr. Shaw's publishers call "vital, modern, poetic prose." There are too many dreary hours between this rosy-fingered dawn and that rosy-fingered dawn. The menaces in ancient Jeopardy were too far apart, the hazards prowled at too great distances, the gods maundered and were repetitious. Ulysses himself is not a hero to whom a young man's fancy turns in any season. The comedy of the *Odyssey* is thought by some students to be unintentional and by others to be intentional, and there must not be any uncertainty about comedy. But whatever may be said about it, the *Odyssey* will always keep bobbing up, in our years and in the years to follow them. The brazen entry into the United States of Mr. Joyce's *Ulysses* has most recently brought the

Odyssey again into view; as the magazine *Time* points out to its surprised readers, "almost every detail of the *Odyssey*'s action can be found in disguised form in *Ulysses*." So, many a reader might naturally enough ask, what? So nothing—that is, nothing of real importance in so far as the *Odyssey* or *Ulysses* itself is concerned. The ancient story just happened to make a point of departure for Mr. Joyce. He might equally well have taken for a pattern Sherman's campaign in Georgia. Nevertheless, here is the old tale before us again not quite two years after Mr. Shaw went over the whole ground for the twenty-eighth time in English.

My purpose in this essay is no such meager and footless one as to suggest that it is high time for some other ancient tale to be brought up in place of the *Odyssey*—although, if urged, I would say the *Morte d'Arthur*. My purpose is to put forward in all sincerity and all arrogance the conviction that the right *Odyssey* has yet to be done, and to name as the man to do it no less a genius than Walt Disney. A year or two ago Mr. Disney made a Silly Symphony, as he too lightly called this masterpiece, entitled "Neptune." Those who missed seeing it missed a lusty, fearsome, beautiful thing. Here was a god and here were sea adventures in the ancient manner as nobody else has given them to us. The thing cannot be described; it can be rendered into no English. But it was only a hint of what Mr. Disney, let loose in the *Odyssey*, could make of it.

The dark magic of Circe's isle, the crossing between Scylla and Charybdis, the slaying of the suitors are just by the way; and so are dozens of other transfigurations, mythical feats of strength, and godly interventions. Mr. Disney could toss these away by the dozen and keep only a select few. For one: Ulysses and his men in the cave of the Cyclops. That would be that scene as I should like my daughter to know it first, when she gets ready for the *Odyssey*, or when she is grimly made ready for it—I presume one still has to read it in school as I did, along with *The Talisman* and *Julius Caesar*. Picture Mr. Disney's version of the overcoming of the giant, the escape tied to the sheep, the rage of Polyphemus as he hurls the tops of mountains at the fleeing ship of Ulysses and his men!

But I think my favorite scene will be (I'm sure Mr. Disney will do the *Odyssey* if we all ask him please) that scene wherein Menelaus and his followers wrestle with the wily Proteus on the island of Pharos. You know: The Old Man of the Sea comes up out of the dark

JAMES THURBER

waters at noon to count his droves of precious seals all stretched out on the beach. In his innocence of treachery or of any change in the daily routine, he unwittingly counts Menelaus and his three men, who are curled up among the seals trying to look as much like seals as possible. It doesn't come out, by the way, in any rendering I've read, and I've read two, just what the Old Man thought when he found he had four seals too many. Anyway, at the proper moment Menelaus and his followers jump upon Proteus. In the terrific struggle that ensues the Old Man changes into—here I follow the Shaw version—"a hairy lion; then a dragon; then a leopard; then a mighty boar. He became a film of water, and afterwards a high-branched tree."

How only for Walt Disney's hand and his peculiar medium was that battle fought! His *Odyssey* can be, I am sure, a far, far greater thing than even his epic of the three little pigs. Let's all write to him about it, or to Roosevelt.

Peace, It's Wonderful

In an extensive reading of recent books by psychologists, psychoanalists, psychiatrists, and inspirationalists, I have discovered that they all suffer from one or more of these expression-complexes: italicizing, capitalizing, exclamation-pointing, multiple-interrogating, and itemizing. These are all forms of what the psychos themselves would call, if they faced their condition frankly, Rhetorical Over-compensation. It is a defense mechanism used to cover up a lack of anything new and sound to say on their favorite subjects, and to make up for an inability to write simply and convincingly, or to think clearly. We find, in all these men and women, the raised voice, and the glib invention that so often accompanies it; we find, too, an easy fancy in place of a sound imagination; hence we are bound to find those broad glittering generalizations, based on any little specific instance which comes to hand, that distinguish the lecturer from the researcher. The desire to help, implicit in the very titles of these books, becomes so often merely the urge to startle.

Dr. Louis E. Bisch, whose book I set out to review, only to find myself turning now and again to some of my other patients because of a striking similarity of symptoms, is an italicizing multiple-interrogator (he has what I like to think of as Billy Sunday's Disease: "Do you think God will let you? *No!* Do you know why He won't let you? *No!* Shall I tell you why?"). This is a typical passage from Dr. Bisch's book: "Do you wonder why I say that *to be normal is nothing to brag* about? The times are out of joint? I agree. But who knocked them out of joint? Besides, are these the first signs of demoralization in history? Can you name an era . . . etc., etc.?" In the first paragraph

EDITOR'S NOTE: A review of *Be Glad You're Neurotic*, by Louis E. Bisch, M.D.

of his Chapter VII he starts off with eight straight questions, possibly a world's record.

I should like to turn for a moment to a few of the doctor's contemporaries in the field of the mind. Mrs. Dorothea Brande, then, is an italicizing capitalizer (her preface to *Wake Up and Live!* is written in italics. She is fond of such capitalizations as "Will to Fail"). Mr. David Seabury, author of five books on "mentation," is an itemizing multiple-interrogator (I turned at random to page 168 of his *How to Worry Successfully* and came to four sentences in succession beginning with questions: "Need we argue . . . ? Why should we not recognize . . . ? Why should we not see . . . ? Is there any reason why . . . ?" In one place he itemizes thirty-three forms of "mentation" and right beside them, thirty-three "varieties of obliquity"). Dr. Walter B. Pitkin is an itemizing italicizer (my favorite of all his italics are these, from his *Psychology of Happiness. "I enjoy the simultaneous flight of a half-dozen trains of ideas, which run on parallel tracks for a certain distance, then disappear, arriving nowhere."* This arriving nowhere of a half-dozen trains of ideas is a characteristic of the mentationists).

I want now to submit an example of expression-complex, or typographical elephantiasis, in its last stages. I quote, exactly, from Mr. George Winslow Plummer's *Consciously Creating Circumstances: "In consciously creating circumstances we reverse the process of physical sight.* Instead of seeing mentally a picture of what we know already exists physically, we use this giant power within us by impressing our individual subjective mind WITH THE PICTURE OF WHAT WE WANT TO SEE COME ABOUT PHYSICALLY." This is an extreme case but it is by no means unique. Let us turn to the last page of Dr. Bisch's book and examine an almost identical condition:

"In any case, *follow these five simple rules.* Remind yourself of them morning and night. If necessary, paste them inside your hat!

STUDY YOURSELF

STOP REPROACHING YOURSELF

BE PROUD OF WHAT YOU ARE

TURN YOUR HANDICAPS INTO ASSETS

PROFIT BY YOUR NEUROSIS

Then

BE GLAD!"

After laying down a book by one of these elated exhorters you have the calming effect of getting out into the open air from a stuffy room in which someone has been shouting at his deaf aunt and bawling out a little child at the same time.

I have neither the space nor the strength to go in detail into Dr. Bisch's chapters, but I should like to quote a few passages, this time for content and not for form. If you want more, there is the Glad Book itself (and on the same counter you will find two dozen others just like it). Here we go: "I am claiming you should be glad you're neurotic. All the great thinkers and doers were glad. Take Alexander the Great, Caesar and Napoleon. Consider Michelangelo, Pascal, Pope, our own Poe, O. Henry, and Walt Whitman." "Fortify yourself against the emotional shock of the unexpected by reading literature and seeing plays and movies that actually depend for interest upon the unexpected. Mystery and detective stories are excellent. Shock yourself often in a vicarious manner and you won't be so shocked when the unexpected of a frightening or even harrowing nature occurs in real life. For the time being it may not make you glad but you surely will be glad later." "A man who *mislays* his hat either dislikes it, wants a new one, experienced unpleasantness when last he wore it, or he does not want to go out." "If a person leaves an umbrella or any other article in your house, you may be sure that he enjoyed his visit and would like to return." And my favorite: "But at least, and at last, sex has been fearlessly roped and thrown." (The marvel is they haven't broken its back.)

This will give you, I think, the flavor of the doctor's message, mystic, wonderful. In the back of his book there is a test you can take to see whether you are neurotic or normal. I came out, in all honesty, 91 per cent normal, which means, for one thing, that I am the kind of person who would have bought—or maybe sold—one of those miniature ladders that were hawked in the streets of Flemington during the Hauptmann trial. It's all right there in Dr. Bisch's book.

JAMES THURBER

Tempest in a Looking Glass

Dr. Paul Schilder, research professor of psychiatry at New York University, has his work cut out for him. I have cut it out for him myself. I hope he is a young man, for there is so much for him to do: What I am about to outline will take him at least ten years, if it is to be done properly.

First, I should perhaps introduce Dr. Paul Schilder to you or, rather, refresh your memory about him. He is the distinguished scientist who, some weeks ago at the Hotel Waldorf-Astoria, analyzed, for the members of the American Psychoanalytic Association in solemn meeting there, the unfortunate nature of the late Charles Lutwidge Dodgson, better known to the world under his escapist pen name of Lewis Carroll. Dr. Schilder had found in his researches, you may remember, that *Alice in Wonderland* is so full of cruelty, fear, and "sadistic trends of cannibalism" that he questioned its wholesomeness as literature for children. (Could it have been *Alice* that debauched the kiddies in Mr. Richard Hughes's *High Wind in Jamaica*? I suggest that Dr. Schilder set about the analysis of Mr. Hughes right now. Maybe *he* was debauched, as a child, by the works of Lewis Carroll.)

Dr. Schilder seems to have been pained and astonished by his belated discovery that everything in *Wonderland* and *Through the Looking Glass* is out of joint. He spoke, according to the report of his lecture in the *New York Times,* of the "unwholesome instability of space" and the "tendency of the time element to be thrown out of gear." He found, in a word, a world of "cruelty, destruction, and annihilation." He also found cruelty inherent in Mr. Carroll's "destructive use of the English language," but that's beside my point, that's something to be fought out, man to man, between Dr. Schilder and some writer younger and stronger than I—I nominate Ernest Hemingway or Jim Tully.

As I said to begin with, I have some further researchers to suggest to Dr. Paul Schilder (after he gets through with the cruel and sadistic Richard Hughes). They will keep him even busier and shock him, I am afraid, even more severely than his work with Mr. Carroll did. I submit to him, as a starting-off place, the *English Fairy Tales* collected so painstakingly 42 years ago by Mr. Joseph Jacobs. With the exception of *The Three Bears,* which was the invention of the cruel and sadistic poet Southey, these are all folk tales. In getting at the bottom of the savagery, the mercilessness, the ferocity, and the sadistic trends of cannibalism of these tales, Dr. Schilder will be able to expose the evil nature not of one man, not of one race of men but of the whole of mankind, for there is, of course, scarcely a story in this compilation which has not its counterpart, parallel, or source in the folk tales of another country. Usually, each story may be traced to a dozen countries, from Ireland to India, from France to Russia, from Germany to Iceland. Let us examine, rather minutely, for Dr. Schilder's enlightenment, just one of these tales, the one entitled by Mr. Jacobs *The Rose-Tree.* Dr. Schilder will surely want to analyze *The Rose-Tree* and the depraved soul of man which shines so darkly behind it.

SHE LAUGHED, DR. SCHILDER!

"There was once upon a time [the tale begins] a good man who had two children: a girl by his first wife, and a boy by the second. The girl was as white as milk, and her lips were like cherries." The tale goes on to tell how the stepmother hated the little girl and one day sent her to the store to buy a pound of candles which, when she put them on the ground while she climbed over a stile, a dog stole. Three times this happened, with three different pounds of candles. "The stepmother was angry, but she pretended not to mind the loss. She said to the child: 'Come, lay your head on my lap that I may comb your hair.' " Down to the ground fell the yellow silken hair as the stepmother combed it. Said she, finally: "I cannot part your hair on my knee, fetch a billet of wood." When this was done she said,

"I cannot part your hair with a comb, fetch me an ax." So (brace yourself, Dr. Schilder, for here comes cruelty which makes the cruelty of Mr. Carroll seem like the extremely lovely nonsense it really is) the stepmother made the little girl put her head upon the billet of wood, and then she cut off her head with the ax. In the tale as Mr. Jacobs tells it there comes now this sentence: "So the mother wiped the ax and laughed." In all of Lewis Carroll, Dr. Schilder, there is no such sentence as that. There, indeed, is grist for your mill; there is red meat for your grinder. But wait. We are coming to a real trend in cannibalism.

"Then she took the heart and liver of the little girl, and she stewed them and brought them into the house for supper. The husband tasted them and shook his head. He said they tasted very strangely. She gave some to the little boy, but he would not eat." The little boy, the story tells, took up what was left of his little sister and put her in a box and buried the box under a rose tree. "And every day he went to the tree and wept and his tears ran down on the box. One day the rose-tree flowered. It was spring, and there among the flowers was a white bird; and it sang, and sang, and sang like an angel out of heaven." The song the bird sang is, in the version Mr. Jacobs uses, this dainty ditty:

> *My wicked mother slew me,*
> *My dear father ate me,*

COLLECTING HIMSELF

My little brother whom I love,
Sits below and I sing above,
Stick, stock, stone dead.

The white bird, the tale goes, sang her song for the shoemaker, and he gave her two little red shoes; and she sang her song for the watchmaker, and he gave her a gold watch and chain; and she sang her song for three millers, and they put, when she asked for it, a millstone around her neck. Then the white bird flew to the house where the stepmother lived. And from there I give the tale as it is in the book, on to the end. "It rattled the millstone against the eaves of the house, and the stepmother said: 'It thunders.' Then the little boy ran out to see the thunder, and down dropped the red shoes at his feet. It rattled the millstone against the eaves of the house once more, and the stepmother said again: 'It thunders.' Then the father ran out, and down fell the chain about his neck. In ran father and son, laughing and saying: 'See, what fine things the thunder has brought us!' Then the bird rattled the millstone against the eaves of the house a third time; and the stepmother said: 'It thunders again, perhaps the thunder has brought something for me," and she ran out; but the moment she stepped outside the door down fell the millstone on her head; and so she died."

Dr. Paul Schilder will want, of course, to trace the extent of this cruel and cannibalistic story among the peoples of the world. To aid him in his quest I should like to quote a paragraph from Mr. Jacobs's notes and references at the end of his book:

SOURCE.—From the first edition of Henderson's *Folk-Lore of Northern Counties*, p. 314, to which it was communicated by the Rev. S. Baring-Gould.

PARALLELS.—This is better known under the title, "Orange and Lemon," and with the refrain:

> *"My mother killed me,*
> *My father picked my bones,*
> *My little sister buried me,*
> *Under the marble stones."*

I heard this in Australia, and a friend of mine heard it in her youth in County Meath, Ireland. Mr. Jones gives part of it in *Folk-Tales of the Magyars*, 418–20, and another version occurs in

Notes and Queries, vi. 496. Mr. I. Gollancz informs me he remembers a version entitled "Pepper, Salt, and Mustard," with the refrain just given. Abroad it is Grimm's "Juniper Tree," where see further parallels. The German rhyme is sung by Margaret in the mad scene of Goethe's *Faust*.

Once launched onto the awful, far-spreading sea of folklore, Dr. Schilder will find a thousand examples, in the fairy tales of all countries, of fear and cruelty, horror and revenge, cannibalism and the laughing wiping of blood from gory axes. He must surely know, to give just one more example, the tale from the brothers Grimm of how a queen "quite yellow with envy" sang to another looking glass than Lewis Carroll's: "O, mirror, mirror on the wall, who is the fairest of us all?" and how, when the mirror answered that the fairest maid alive was the queen's own stepdaughter, Snow White, the enraged lady sent for a huntsman and said to him: "Take the child away into the forest. . . . You must kill her and bring me her heart and tongue for a token."

OF ART AND OUR PSYCHOLOGISTS

Dr. Schilder's work, as I have said, is cut out for him. He has the evil nature of Charles Perrault to dip into, surely as black and devious and unwholesome as Lewis Carroll's. He has the Grimms and Hans Christian Andersen. He has Mother Goose, or much of it. He can spend at least a year on the legend of Childe Rowland, which is filled with perfectly swell sexual symbols—from (in some versions) an underground cave more provocative by far than the rabbit hole in Wonderland to the sinister Dark Tower of the more familiar versions. This one piece of research will lead him into the myth of Proserpine and into Browning and Shakespeare and Milton's *Comus* and even into the dark and perilous kingdom of Arthurian legend. I should think that the good doctor could spend a profitable month on the famous and mysterious beast Galtisant, that was called the Questing Beast and that so plagued Sir Palamides—"the Questing Beast that had in shape a head like a serpent's head, and a body like a leopard, buttocks like a lion, and footed like an hart; and in his body there was such a noise as it had been the noise of thirty couple

of hounds questing, and such a noise that beast made whereso-
mever he went."

When he is through with all this, Dr. Schilder should be pretty
well persuaded that behind the imaginative works of all the cruel
writing men, further or nearer, lies the destructive and unstable, the
fearful and unwholesome, the fine and beautiful cruelty of the peoples of the earth, the men and women in the fields and the huts and
the market place, the original storytellers of this naughty world. If
Dr. Schilder wishes to expose to the members of the American Psychoanalytic Association, at some far date, the charming savagery and
the beautiful ruthlessness of these peoples of the world, these millions
long dead—and still alive—that is up to him. I should protest mildly
that there is much more important work to be done.

I had planned, to be sure, a small analysis and defense of the
nature of the artistic imagination for Dr. Schilder's information.
Thinking of this one afternoon, I stood at a window of my house in
the country, and as I looked out three pheasants came walking across
the snow, almost up to my window. They were so near that, if I had
had a stout rubber band and a ruler to snap it from, I could have got
one of them. Presently they wandered away, and with them, somehow, went my desire to explain the nature of the artistic imagination,
in my humble way, to Dr. Paul Schilder. But I should like to leave
with him, to ponder, one little definition, the definition of the word
empathy as given in *Webster's New International Dictionary:* "Imaginative projection of one's own consciousness into another human being;
sympathetic understanding of other than human beings." There's a
great deal in that—for some people—Dr. Schilder.

And, at the far end of all this tempest in a looking glass, I should
like to set down, for Paul Schilder's guidance, a sentence from the
writings of the late Dr. Morton Prince, a truly intelligent psychologist. He was speaking of multiple personality when he wrote it but
he might have been speaking of the folk tales of the world or of the
creatures and creations of Lewis Carroll: "Far from being mere
freaks, monstrosities of consciousness, they are in fact shown to be
manifestations of the very constitution of life."

JAMES THURBER

Voices of Revolution

The old bitter challenges to the bourgeois as critic, writer, and human being (in answer to the old bitter challenges of the bourgeois to the proletarian as critic, writer, and human being) ring out right at the start in Joseph Freeman's introduction to *Proletarian Literature in the United States.* Nothing, I am afraid, will ever change this. We shall all meet at the barricades shouting, or writing, invective at the top of our voices. Interspersed, of course, with sound arguments (to which the other side will not listen). The bourgeois writer and critic and the proletarian writer and critic do not seem to be able to meet, sanely, on a forum. Their meeting place is the battlefield. They are cat and dog, Smith and Roosevelt. This cannot, I suppose, be changed and it is a rather melancholy reflection. Out of it are bound to come distortion, exaggeration, and, what is probably worse, triviality. But it presents a colorful, if meaningless, free-for-all, which members of both armies, being human beings born of war, are bound to find rather more pleasurable than deplorable.

Mr. Freeman sets himself a large and important task in his introduction and, in great part, he discharges it well, the great part being an explanation of, and argument for, the values of revolutionary art. But here and there the old urge springs up, the old bitter desire to take irrelevant cracks at bourgeois literature (without specific instances), and at the more intimate emotions of the bourgeoisie, all the more intimate emotions of all the bourgeoisie. He hates to use the word "love" in relation to them. Thus he speaks of "lechery" and of

EDITOR'S NOTE: A review of *Proletarian Literature in the United States,* edited by Granville Hicks.

"flirtations"; when he does use the word "lovers" he joins it up with "loafers." This petty bitterness—it seems almost a neurosis—disfigures his arguments. He writes:

> Every writer creates not only out of his feelings, but out of his knowledge and his concepts and his will. . . . The feelings of the proletarian writer are molded by his experience and by the science which explains that experience, just as the bourgeois writer's feelings are molded by his experiences and the class theories which rationalize them. Out of the experiences and the science of the proletariat the revolutionary poets, playwrights and novelists are developing an art which reveals more forces in the world than the love of the lecher and the pride of the Narcissist.

Well, there you are: the old slipping out of a sonorous and imposing argument into what is nothing more than a hot-tempered jibe, a silly sweeping insinuation. It is odd how that kind of thing has somehow or other become one of the major points in the literary battle. Studies of the effects of class backgrounds and social concepts upon the emotions belong in such works as *Middletown,* or in articles by themselves, but they should scarcely be flung helter-skelter into an analysis of the kind Mr. Freeman sets out to write, particularly if they degenerate into what has the thin ring of an absurd personal insult. So much of the critical writing of both proletarians and bourgeoisie sounds as if the writer were striking back at some individual who has been striking at him. I am afraid that is too often the case. Schoolgirls; boys behind the barn. And literature can go die, on the barricades, or behind the barn.

But this is not getting into the book, which is divided into Fiction, Poetry, Reportage (that's what they call it, don't look at me), Drama, and Literary Criticism. It runs to 384 pages. It contains selections from the work of proletarian writers in the past five or six years. I have read it with great interest and I believe anybody with any sense of what is going on would also. I was mainly interested in the fiction; first, because it takes up more than a third of the volume; second, because, of the five divisions, I care most for fiction.

The fiction here I found uneven: sincere generally, sometimes groping, often hysterical or overwrought, now and then distinctly moving. The only thing in this section that I think can last is John Dos Passos's "The Body of an American" from *1919.* Many of the other authors have the fault of whipping themselves up to a lather, or whipping their characters up to a lather, whereas Dos Passos whips his reader up to a lather. Somewhere in this book there should be a critical piece on his method. It might well have been put in, under Literary Criticism, in place of Mr. Gold's famous attack on Thornton Wilder, which seems as dated as the Dempsey-Carpentier fight, or in place of Phillips's and Rahv's "Recent Problems of Revolutionary Literature," which loses its points in a mass of heavy, difficult, and pedantic writing. For what some of these proletarian writers need to learn is simply how to write, not only with intensity, but with conviction, not only with a feeling for the worker but a feeling for literary effects. Even the Erskine Caldwell of "Daughter" (by which flabby story he is unfortunately represented here) might learn from Dos Passos. Compare (and you'll have to read both pieces to see the really important difference) Caldwell's refrain: "Daughter woke up hungry again. . . . I just couldn't stand it" with Dos Passos's: "Say buddy cant you tell me how I can get back to my outfit?" The first flops, the second gets you.

Many of the stories are simply not convincing. I have read several two or three times to see if I could discover why. I think I found a few reasons. You don't always believe that these authors *were there,* ever had been there; that they ever saw and heard these people they write about. They give you the feeling that they are writing what they want these people to have said. This seems to me an important point. It is not the subject matter, but the method of presentation, I believe, which has raised the bourgeois cry of "propaganda." Proletarian literature must be written by men and women with a keen ear and eye for gestures and for words, for mannerisms and for idioms, or it fails. Jack Conroy catches perfectly the words of the Negro in his "A Coal Miner's Widow" (particularly in the fine paragraph on page 58 beginning " 'Scuse me!"); but I don't feel reality—I vaguely feel some literary influence—in most of Ben Field's "Cow." And he should be forever ashamed of having written this sentence: "He said something about her being without either and without clothes, but for the sake of somebody who liked him, as he had been unable to get her off, he had had all added." But then read his "The Cock's

Funeral" in the first issue of *Partisan Review* and *Anvil;* it is fine, and it has what nothing in this anthology has: humor. Some of the richest humor in the world is the humor of the American proletariat.

I think Albert Halper fails to make his scab taxi-driver come to life. I did not believe the driver and I did not believe his fares; I believed Mr. Halper's sincerity; and that is not enough. More care and hard work, in watching and listening and writing, is what was needed here. The driver is not nearly so good as Joseph North's driver in his reporter piece called "Taxi Strike," and Mr. North's study is far from excellent. I believe both Halper and North might profit by an examination into the way Robert Coates or St. Clair McKelway handles such pieces. I can tell you that their observation and their writing is hard, painstaking, and long. Nobody, however greatly aroused, can successfully bat off anything.

Now I *did* believe Albert Maltz's "Man on a Road" (minor note: I am told that no user of "you-all" ever addresses a solitary person as "you-all"). This story is written with sympathy and understanding but also with detachment (and oh, my friends, and oh, my foes, in detachment there is strength, not weakness). Mr. Maltz leaves the clear plight of his victim undefiled by exaggeration, anger, and what I can only call the "editorial comment" which seeps into some of the other pieces. You remember the man on the road after you have forgotten most of the figures in the book. Mr. Maltz knows how to make his reader angry without demanding that he be angry. And if this is not the procedure of class, it will forever remain the dictate of art.

I thought that the dialogue in Grace Lumpkin's "John Stevens" had an artificial sound—one gets to thinking more about the writer than about her people, more about her faults than about what is troubling her characters. I can understand why the Communist literati bewail the loss to the cause of Ring Lardner—as they should also bewail the straying of John O'Hara. In this kind of story an ear like theirs is worth more than rubies. To go on: there is too obvious strain and effort in Tillie Lerner; she grabs tremendously at the reader and at life and fails to fetch the reader and fails to capture life. William Rollins Jr. has a deplorable affection for typographical pyrotechnics: caps, italics, dashes. It makes his story almost impossible to read. I was reminded, in trying to read it, of what an old English professor of mine, the late Joseph Russell Taylor, used to say: you can't get passion into a story with exclamation points. But Mr. Rollins deserves credit for one thing, at least: he is the only writer in this book who uses "God damn" in place of "goddam." Josephine Herbst, so often authentic, writes: "A newsboy sang out, 'Big Strike at Cumley's, night crew walk out, big strike threatened, mayor urges arbitration.' " That is what she wanted to hear a newsboy sing out but it is not what any newsboy in this country ever sang out. I grant the importance of the scenes on which all these stories are based, but they cannot have reality, they cannot be literature, if they are slovenly done—merely because there is a rush for the barricades and proletarian writers are in a hurry. Art does not rush to the barricades. Nobody wants to believe that these authors sat in warm surroundings hurriedly writing of things they had never seen, or had merely glimpsed, yet that is often the impression they give.

At the end of the fiction section is the worst example of failure in method and effect, Philip Stevenson's "Death of a Century." What might have been sharp satire is a badly done, overwrought, and merely gross burlesque. Even burlesque must keep one foot on verisimilitude. It grows better out of healthy ridicule than wild-eyed hate. In the poetry and drama departments there are fine things (*Waiting for Lefty* among them). The reportage section is, in some instances, excellent and it should have been widely expanded, preferably at the expense of the literary criticism, almost all of which could have been left out. There is, as I have said, not a note of humor in the anthology, not even in Robert Forsythe's piece on the Yale Bowl.

"This is my brother Ed. He's given up."

"Don'ts" for the Inflation

Don't shout over the phone

Don't run

JAMES THURBER

Don't lie down

COLLECTING HIMSELF

Don't keep saying "Hark!"

Don't scream

JAMES THURBER

Don't offer money you printed yourself

Notes for a
Proletarian Novel

Back in the nineties, a novelist practically *had* to write novels about a gentleman standing at the top of a flight of stairs with a sword in his hand, his shirt open at the throat, and a bandage around his forehead, defending some lady's honor. These novels were not proletarian any way you looked at them, and they pay the penalty of seeming pretty dim and futile now. In fact, they may be said to be quite dead, along with Stanley Weyman and that long line of gallant French swordsmen which began with D'Artagnan and ended when Frenchmen began throwing rocks at gendarmes on May Day.

The next type of popular novel to come into vogue, as I remember it, had for its protagonist a tall, gaunt, melancholy author whose story involved his lifelong and unsuccessful search for Something Worth While. This he mainly sought for in women, and women always failed him because they turned out, much to his surprise, not to be God, Beauty, and Inspiration all in one. They turned out to be saucy and irritable at times, with no clearer understanding of what the protagonist was searching for than he had, so that in the end he wandered sadly off into the dusk, without a hat on, his lank hair blowing across his face, still searching. These novels were not proletarian either, and they seem pretty silly now in a world that is no longer safe for Individualism.

Then there was a period when a thin white line of ironic and satirical novels was thrown upon the shore. These novels made fun of Everything, in a nicely polished way, but you can't do that any more because Everything has become sombre and important in the last few years. Authors privileged to live in this age must write novels about the workingman, with a drab economic background—and don't let me see any of you sneaking into fine old Edith Wharton drawing-rooms. The tone of critics of literature is becoming sharper and more threatening as time goes on and not enough proletarian novels come out. There is a hint implicit in literary reviews that unless authors give up monkeying around with well-to-do characters who fritter their time away on Love, something is going to happen. There is no place for Love any more, either.

As much as I care about Individualism and Love, I'm not so dumb but what I see that I'll have to settle down to a book about factory life if I'm going to keep up with the times. Unfortunately, the only factory I was ever in in my life was the Buckeye Steel Castings Company, in Columbus, Ohio, and that was so many years ago that I can't remember a thing except that I stumbled over a big iron bucket and was lame for days. My other contacts with the working class have also been pretty slight, but I remember a few of them.

When I was sixteen, I used to work for a wealthy and bureaucratic wholesale optical-supply company in Columbus. I delivered lenses and frames to opticians about town, for twelve dollars a week, making my rounds on a bicycle. I suppose that I was pretty much ground down by the capitalistic system then, but I didn't give it much thought because I was working at the time on the development of a baseball game to be played with a pair of dice. A few years later, during my senior year in high school, I got a job working after hours in a small tobacco store on Mt. Vernon Avenue. A great many workingmen came into the store, which was run by a man named Una Soderblom. Most of the patrons were employees of the Pennsylvania Railroad Company—engineers, firemen, and brakemen. My memory of their problems is dim, but I think that their greatest one was waking up in time to get to their trains. Often they turned over and went back to sleep after being telephoned by the official Caller. I could do the character of the Caller, all right. He was a slight grayish man who never wore a collar, but always wore a back collar button anyway, and he sat at a table with a telephone on it in the rear of the store. Just why his office was in the tobacco shop I never found out. He studied in his spare time what he called "Physic." Physic was, in reality, the science of psychic phenomena, especially hypnotism. Most of the engineers and firemen scoffed at his studies, but there was one fireman named McCready who was a pushover for the Caller. The Caller used to hypnotize McCready every time he came into the store. He would do this by spinning a small top on one of the glass cigar counters, and make the fireman stare at it; then he would speak to him in a low, commanding voice and McCready would stiffen all over and begin to flop around as if he were a mechanical fireman instead of a live one. Most of the engineers who saw these performances were not very crazy about making runs with McCready. Another interesting character was an engineer who could spit fifteen feet, and there was a fireman who had been runner-up for two successive years in the speed races of the Central Ohio Ice Skating Carnival. I remember one day he came into the shop and said he had just bought a blue suit "with a red stripe into it." And that's all I got out of my experience with railroad workers. In those days I didn't think much about the plight of the workingman, if, indeed, I knew that he had one, and anyway I was elected president of my senior class at high school while I was working at the shop, which made me feel superior to everybody that came into the place, even Mr. Soderblom.

Then when I was about twenty-three and going to the University, I got a summer-time job with an organization in Columbus known as the State-City Free Employment Agency. This brought me into contact with the working classes again, but I didn't think anything at the time about studying their conditions and I can only remember a few things that happened. One day an unemployed cleaning woman came into the office and applied for housework. I asked her what kind of housework she wanted and she looked at me steadily and, I thought, disapprovingly for a long time. "Young man, are you saved?" she asked me. I lied and said that I was, but she obviously didn't think so and went away dissatisfied with the way the agency was run. "What did you say to that woman?" demanded my superior, walking over to my desk. "She asked me if I was saved and I told her I was," I said. He bit off the end of a stogy. "Never mind about that," he said. "Git 'em work. Git 'em work."

These constitute my principal experiences with the problems of the working classes, and they are not enough. I did have, to be sure, also some slight connection with the recent waiters' strike in this city, as a member of a committee interested in their welfare, but I was

JAMES THURBER

pretty much overshadowed by the presence on the committee of three novelists, a columnist, and a painter. I became fairly familiar, however, with the problem of the waiters, but I doubt very much whether I could make a novel out of it. In the first place, I haven't the slightest idea what waiters do when they go home. I have simply no picture at all of what they do at home, and an author cannot omit the home life of his characters from his novels. I could probably never bring myself to the point of asking a waiter to invite me to his home, because I always get tightened up in the presence of waiters. The only one I was ever at ease with was a waiter at the Waldorf whom I bought a drink for during the Cinderella Ball, mistaking him for an artist. I found out he was a waiter when he wouldn't sit down. I wouldn't know what to do if a waiter who was my host at his own house brought me a cocktail and didn't sit down while I was drinking it. I suppose he would sit down, but I don't know. No waiter ever has sat down with me, and I wouldn't know what would be the thing to do if one did. Stand up, maybe. You couldn't tip a waiter unless one of you stood up.

I am pretty well persuaded by now that I am not the man to write a proletarian novel. Of course, there is always the drama, but that is just as difficult for me. I have tried a couple of plays and I always run into appalling problems. One of these is that my plays are always over at the end of the first act. There is never any reason in the world any of the characters should ever see each other again. Another problem is that although the people I put in plays talk quite glibly, they don't do anything. They just sit there. I once wrote a whole act in which nobody moved. The expedient of going back over such an act and having the characters shift from chair to sofa and back again, smoking cigarettes, is not much of a help.

It is also extremely difficult to get characters on and off the stage dexterously. It may look easy, but it isn't easy. I have frequently had to resort to dogfights. "I must go out and separate those dogs" is not, however, a sound or convincing exit line for someone you have to get off the stage. Furthermore, you can only use the dogfight device once unless the dogs are total strangers who have been tied up together in the back yard, and that would have to be explained. You can't explain the relationship of two dogs, particularly two dogs your audience hasn't seen, in less than thirty seconds, and thirty seconds is a long time in the theatre. Percy Hammond would write that the play was a noisy prank which nobody need go to see if he has anything else to do at all.

So there goes my play, too, probably. I don't know what Mr. Granville Hicks will think of me. Mr. Hicks is one of the literary critics who most stoutly demand that all novels and plays be proletarian in theme, and all poems, too, as far as that goes. He believes that Emily Dickinson failed miserably in her lyrics about bees because she didn't give any serious attention to the problem of the workers. My God, does anybody think drones are happy?

JAMES THURBER

Ave Atque Vale

Three friends of mine, all of them writers, died this summer, for I have reached the time of life when a man's contemporaries begin to drift away like autumn leaves, having attained their highest development and fullest color. One of these three was Carl Van Doren, distinguished friend, historian, teacher, editor, critic, and biographer of Benjamin Franklin. In his honor more than two hundred of the thousands of persons who knew, loved, and admired him gathered in New York in September. Such a meeting is likely to be marked by the kind of solemnity that grows out of reverence, and leads to tribute, estimate, and appraisal.

It came to me, sitting and listening to the warmly affectionate words of half a dozen of his closest friends and colleagues, that garments of praise must be inevitably cut in such a fashion as to fit several or even many individuals almost equally well, and that only the personal anecdote about a man is uniquely his own, and can be worn by no one else at all. There were not enough anecdotes about Carl Van Doren that night, since remembrance of glow and radiance is likely to create generalization. Clifton Fadiman, however, told of the time that Carl was asked to define a classic. "A classic is a book that doesn't have to be written again," said Mr. Van Doren. One of the speakers was Mary Margaret McBride, and of all the excellent memoirs, hers was one of the best, but she forgot to tell something that "my favorite man in all the world" had said one day on her radio program.

She asked him that day if it was hard to write. "Yes, it's hard to write," he said, "but it's harder not to." Carl had a fine talent for the off-hand but profound truth which is always made up in equal parts of fact and wit or humour. His statement about writing belongs in my private collection of rare items, along with Robert Benchley's observation that the free-lance writer is a man who is paid per piece or per word or perhaps.

My own favorite anecdote about Carl Van Doren takes me back nearly twenty years, or a decade before I came to know him personally. I had gone to Town Hall in New York, accompanied by a young lady, to listen to a debate on Humanism in which Mr. Van Doren was one of the participants, along with Henry Seidel Canby, the late Irving Babbitt, and others. Carl was the last speaker called on, and during the arguments of the others, my companion had been restless to the point of plain inattention. Then Carl stood up. Before he could speak a word, she turned to me and said warmly, "I'm on *his* side!" She wanted me to take her up to meet him when the debate was over, but I was too timid. "I just want to see him long enough to tell him I love him," she said. Ten years later I told Carl about the incident one night at a party and he said, with his likeable smile, "Every man is entitled to meet the women that love him." I think he did meet her. I have known very few people since I came to New York twenty-five years ago whom he didn't know. None of them will ever forget him.

JAMES THURBER

Recollections
of Henry James

In almost every autobiography that I have picked up in the past four or five years, there has been a chapter devoted to reminiscences and impressions of Henry James. So I am going to give *mine,* even though this is not an autobiography, and even though I never met Henry James. An author must be "in the swim." I feel that I can at least do as well as Mrs. Atherton does in her *Adventures of a Novelist,* for on one occasion she couldn't make out what he was saying, and the only other time she ever met him she did make out what he was saying but doesn't remember what it was.

Although I never met Henry James, I attended (or we'll say that I did) a party one time at which he told the plot of *The Bat,* the mystery play then very popular and attracting a great deal of attention. One was really not supposed to tell how the play "came out," for this would impair the pleasure of persons who had not yet seen it and who wanted to; I forget now whether it was also supposed to impair the pleasure of those who had not seen it and who had no intention of seeing it, but I suspect that it was: in those days, people's pleasure was pretty easily impaired. There were a few persons at the party who knew how the play came out but hadn't seen it, and a few others who had seen it and still didn't know how it came out. Most of us, however, had not seen it and didn't much care how it came out.

James's great gift, of course, was his ability to tell a plot in shimmering detail with such delicacy of treatment and such fine aloofness—that is, reluctance to engage in any direct grappling with what, in the play or story, had actually "taken place"—that his listeners often did not, in the end, know what had, to put it in another way, "gone on." This made his recital of *The Bat* one of the most remarkable afternoons of my life. Just as, having worked up to a circumstantial arrangement of characters in a concrete situation, he was about to distill some essence of that situation, about, in fine, to pluck from it some fruit into which one could get one's teeth, he would go back and untangle for us the glittering, undulating skein with which he had, at the very beginning, wrapped up the so important (to him) *donnée,* the so charmingly perfect seed, or note absolute, of the story-salient.

There was finally for all of us, at long last, I think, the blurred conviction that the Master had either departed, somewhere in the midst of his beautifully modulated periods, from any further consideration of the play which he had started out to describe, or that he had "worked up to," for his conclusion, the curtain of the *second* act rather than the curtain of the final act, having approached the centre, or "grain," of the story idea from both the beginning and the end, alternately. Which method had the effect, for us, of his having left, fragilely frozen upon the stage, in gestures at once provocative and meaningless, a group of characters, heavy with aborted action, whom he had been causing to spin dreamily around in a circle, like the richly colored figures upon the dial of some old Swiss music box. The brilliant revolution of these marionettes ended at last and whatever "point" Henry James may have intended to make trailed away like mist in the sunlight, leaving us only the unforgettable image of the great placid gentleman talking quietly on and on, never having got anywhere, never, indeed, having, for the matter of that, "come from" anywhere. We had watched him create for us, on the point of a needle, a gleaming and gracious hour, peopled richly with the most sensitive and aware characters, whose evanishment into thin air left us somehow with the feeling that we had become inextricably entangled forever with a group of persons who, while they had never for a moment existed, nevertheless left us, in their departure, with an emptiness that nothing ever again in this world could quite "make up for."

I do not recall now how James happened to get started on *The Bat,* and in justice to the Master it is only fair to say that I am not quite sure that it really was *The Bat* which he gave us that afternoon. It does not now, nor did it then, make any special difference. It was not what Henry James had to say, nor yet the way he said it, that counted; it was something else: I don't know what. Conrad was there and he was, as always, spellbound by the Master's genius. "By God," he would exclaim, "there was never anything like this!" Stevie Crane was not so engrossed; he stood, dark and sombre, in a corner of the room, lassoing, with a rope he had made of the fronds of some potted plants, the necks of vases and the tops of lamps.

All the people that you read about in autobiographies were there, too: W. H. Hudson, Edward Garnett, Miss Hurlbird and her sister, Maurice Hewlett, Ford Madox Ford, S. S. McClure, Ezra Pound, H.D., Æ, T.R., Gilbert Cannan, Hugh Walpole, Arnold Bennett, Sir Edmund Gosse, Chauncey Depew, Joseph H. Choate, Nance O'Neil, Ambrose Bierce, William Gerhardi, Hugh Kingsmill, Richard Le Gallienne, William Randolph Hearst, Lily Langtry, Gene Tunney, Sir Hubert Wilkins, Count von Luckner, Richard Watson Gilder, Robert Underwood Johnson, Elihu Root, Jacob A. Riis, Fremont Older, Albert Jay Nock, Lyman Gage, Ben Lindsey, Doug and Mary Fairbanks, Arthur Brisbane, etc. How all these raconteurs ever let James get started I do not know, unless it was that James was, as you might say, always started in the sense that he had never, at any time, quite ended. As I recall it, one of those present, Mr. Choate, did manage to get in at least one of his anecdotes, even while James was "running on." They sat in adjacent chairs, and their voices, if not the sense of their separate narratives, blended surprisingly well. Choate's story dealt with a time in his career when, without funds, he found himself stranded in New Orleans. "Not wishing to stay longer in the Southern city," said Choate, "for I felt that my opportunities lay elsewhere, I began to think of schemes for getting out of town, all of which, however, were frustrated by the fact that I did not have enough money to take a train or a boat northward. One day I encountered an old colored gentleman named Sam, to whom I explained my plight. 'Why'n you-all steal a rowboat some night and row no'th?' asked Sam. 'By mawnin' you-all'd be in Canada, dat's wheah.' 'Dat's wheah I'd be, huh?' I said, diplomatically falling into his idiom and accent, but by no means won over to a plan of escape which necessitated the stealing of a rowboat. Eventually, it was decided that Sam, and not myself, should steal the rowboat and row to Canada during the night. It was now Sam's turn to be reluctant, but I was firm. 'Look heah, man,' I said. 'You-all proceed discreetly to de ribber jist she gittin' dahk, and having selected a rowboat, git in an' row no'th; by mawnin' you-all absolutely certain to be in Canada.' He still temporized, but in the end decided to act on my judgment. The next morning, just as dawn was breaking, I slipped down to the river to see whether Sam had actually taken a boat and rowed north. To my astonishment, there sat Sam in the dim light mightily rowing a boat which he had neglected to unfasten from the dock and which accordingly had not moved an inch! He had been rowing all night long without getting anywhere. I could hardly believe my eyes. 'Why, hello, Sam!' I shouted at him, finally. He looked slowly over his drooping shoulder, through the mist of early morning. 'Who knows me up heah?' he asked."

In the general laughter that followed, Henry James's voice droned right on: "She had been, as I have said, made, first of all, to I might almost say 'feel,' as indeed so had we all, an incapacity for that way of pleasurable residence within the walls of a house for which my companion had—oh, so rightly!—the word 'contentment,' this incapacity beautifully growing out of what I shall describe as a 'warning' which the poor dear lady had 'received,' all in a by no means restrained flutter, if I may say flutter; I rather thought that the dear lady, to put, for its effect on me, a slightly more 'wingish' word, flapped—"

"By God," said Conrad, "there was never anything like this!" Conrad had the most genuine and unaffected admiration for the Old Man's magic use of words. I think Conrad felt that in his own novels he had made things too preposterously clear and that too many things happened. I remember once he jumped up from a couch on which he had been reading James's "The Beast in the Jungle" and cried, "By God, there was never anything like this! The Old Fellow has actually told a story about a man to whom nothing at all happens! It makes my own Lord Jim, to whom everything at all happens, seem to rush about in a meaningless squirrel-cage of Occurrence!" It was weeks before I could calm him down, before I could dissuade him from a monstrous idea that had taken possession of him; namely, to write a novel in which not only nothing happened but in which there were no characters.

JAMES THURBER

I do not remember exactly how that remarkable afternoon ended. It seems to me, however, that Choate, by biding his time and resting up between anecdotes, was able to finish some few moments after James had ceased talking. "There is now, I brought out for my companion, nothing for us but to leave the theatre," said James, in ending his story. "To which she—oh, so wonderfully—replied, 'Oh.' " "He told me," said Choate, "to call him a cab. 'Very well, sir,' I said, 'you're a cab.' " Conrad reached for his hat. "By God," he said, "there never will be anything like this again!"

The Preface to
"The Old Friends"

(After re-reading some of Henry James's Prefaces, and pre-visioning, as who should say, what might have caught the Master's acute ear and eager fancy at some American party or other in these so disturbed and disturbing present years.)

In touching once again with my mind the beautiful terror of "The Old Friends," I was instantly and with the greatest of sharpnesses confronted with the evoked figure of the poor dear lady with whose predicament my hostess of a long lost afternoon had been so prettily and intensely concerned as to cry out, in my fortunate hearing, "Ah, but doesn't every husband, upon being asked by his wife to bring her a facial tissue, return, after a moment, with a clump of at least fifteen or twenty!" It had seemed to me, promptly enough, that this was the secret door to a moment of privacy and, indeed, intimacy through whose keyhole no gentleman of sensibility should permit himself the briefest of glimpses, and I had accordingly withdrawn to another corner of the lawn and the company of one I shall call Stephen Overleaf, with no disposition whatever to make an enchantment of my hostess's remarkable exclamation or further to pursue her singular fragment of reassurance in any way at all. Alas, I had been conditioned by so many happy decades of devotion to the small trade, if I may so denominate it, of turning a few accidentally overheard words, in this instance twenty-eight, for the sake of exactitude, into a glimmering scene, equipped with all the properties and personae of drama, that I was destined, or, if you will, doomed, to carry the

JAMES THURBER

96

thing like a shining sword which grew and grew in length and brightness during my few minutes of pretending, I must confess it, an attentiveness to whatever poor Overleaf may have been trying to communicate.

The husband with the embarrassing burden of facial tissues would be, it had come to me, not in any sense senile or even senescent, but a gentleman of known, perhaps renowned, taste and sensitivity, whose sudden appearance, in the midst, let us say, of an elegant assemblage of ladies and gentlemen of quality, or of such as now remains, with nearly one-sixth of the entire contents of a container of tissues, would have the effect, not of a tiny helpful domestic gesture, but, I saw it in all clarity, of a dreadful symptom of some gradual but enormous dissolution. It had been my good fortune, since fact has a habit, almost a style, of standing in the way of fiction, not to have caught the name of the poor dear lady who had found herself, perhaps more than once, so overladen with a superabundance of absorbancy, if I may so describe her special plight. Thus I was left with nothing more ponderable than the purest possible speculation, out of which the artifice of my craft produces its sometimes interminable proliferations. I had been on the point of turning away from Overleaf to join a small group of friends on another part of the lawn when, ever so much to my dismay, he complicated the purity of my design by mentioning the name of the poor encumbered lady, which was, for my dissembling purposes, Edith, and adding to this identification a minuscule key of his own in the words, "You have heard, of course, about the dilemma of poor Longstreth, or rather the quandary into which his dilemma has placed John Blaker?" I am, to be sure, supplying these names out of the sheerest fancy, since my concern was, as ever, not with what was actually happening to any living person, but with the fits and starts of my own creative agility. Nonetheless, it seems advisable to throw in a tiny gleam of fact at this juncture, since one had, in truth, popped into my awareness with Overleaf's interrogation. John Blaker, poor Edith's husband, was, then, in his true identity, a writer of considerable achievement, in whose company I had occasionally lingered, but never actually dwelt, the first quite long enough, however, to have caught the tail end of a truth about him which was to be enlarged, by my prying curiosity, into the very crux of my delightful project. Blaker had, like some 90 per cent of the writers I have known or met in these hysterical years, but recently gone into what is over-lightly and vulgarly alluded to as a "tail-spin" or "nose-dive," the pressures of authorship and of peaceful coexistence and of domestic and neural upset having taken their steady toll of his psychological balance. There had come a time, now misty in my remembrance, for the chronology of actuality is ever out of joint with the clock of creativity, and such small realities of the case as came into my possession were soon integrated into my private scheme of elaboration, when poor Blaker had found himself turning in desperation to the one solid rock to which he felt he could in all security cling, his good wife having reverted, as the result of pressures of her own, into the disconsolate period of her first marriage. She had, in fine, taken to addressing poor Blaker not as John, but as Gregory, and this had operated to persuade our friend that he was, in short, losing his grip and identity. In such a situation it is of the very fabric of the writing man to turn to his particular Rock of Ages for solace and reassurance, to be bolstered by the comforting knowledge that at least one person in a crazy world has not yet gone crazy himself. This one person, it must now shine out for my readers, as it still continues to glow, in spite of the years between for me, [was] the figure I have designated as Herbert Longstreth.

The sense which inevitably came to me, literally took me by storm, that my central most dolorous figure was not to be poor dear Edith, nor yet her beshrewed mate, but Herbert Longstreth, had taken me by the throat a moment after I had, with the customary gracious twaddle, thanked my hostess for a pleasant afternoon and had made my homeward way alone down a darkling avenue. The prospect that fairly glittered for me, that would have outdone the sun in radiance had there been a sun to outdo, was the gratifying, the joyful one of so entangling the urgent necessities of Blaker's hope of saving himself with the stealthy but monstrous decline of Longstreth as a possible haven and sanctuary that, in the end, they must both be magnificently lost in a veritable labyrinth of chaotic inability to "get through" to each other and establish even a glimmer of recognition or of old relationships. The impact of this forlorn prefiguration had the effect of so vastly overwhelming me with dejection that I was on the point of abandoning the whole pattern, but in the extremity of age I long ago discovered that such a letting go is not long to be contemplated, and I set about that dramatization of incidents of which

JAMES THURBER

"The Old Friends" is, I have the vanity to protest, so compactly made up.

That what I may be privileged to call the "perspicuity of impinge-ment," the attainment of perfection of focus, if you will, has become more and more difficult with the weathering of the years, may be put down, first of all, to the pressures and stresses of our confused and confusing middle-century and, secondly, oh, indubitably, to the sim-ple chronological truth that my experience of my own species has extended, so to measure it, from the Battle of Fredericksburg to the advent of the hydrogen bomb. Thus, the setting off of the small phenomenon of too many tissues from ever so many thousands of other manifestations of peculiarity stored in my memory, acted at first to deter, yet once again, the compulsive nagging of the drama that was forming in my mind. It seemed, at the earliest of junctures, all but impossible to find a "soundness" of character and incident against which I should be able to play my dreadful show of dissolution. What I am hovering about here, what I am quite reluctant to expose in the barest of terms, is the shaking truth that there is no dependable soundness any longer in the manners and motives of a species whose ultimate goal seems to be that of achieving a cruising speed that will shatter the radiance barrier. Nonetheless, and ever so slowly, I found myself conceiving of a sequence of meetings between Blaker and Longstreth, during which it should almost imperceptibly transpire that neither one has, from the very outset, actually "placed" the other. This abominable but, you must grant me, utterly delicious meaninglessness of contact and communication presented one quite formidable fear, the fear of setting down dialogue into which my readers might never be able, even for the briefest moment, to get their teeth. In such a monstrous contingency, it was dazzlingly clear to me that the central dissolution might be that of myself as narrator. I had magnificently survived the human eccentricities and peculiari-ties of the age of the four-wheeler, the strains of which had been scarcely more than vexatious owing to the blessed circumstance that nothing whatever, more disconcerting than the untoward, had hap-pened during the somnolent decades of the walking stick and the hansom cab. But I was to reach for my effects, in the tortured case of poor dear Longstreth and poor dear Blaker, in an atmosphere of aberration, fixation, compulsion, hallucination, and com—I do abhor the word—plexes. If I should slip off my rocker, to name the major danger vulgarly, I wondered how, in the name of all that was merciful, I should be able to find my way, quite simply, back.

I shall not, for the benefit of such first readers as may wish to be taken by surprise, name or number in all their exquisite detail the threads and textures of my little puzzle, but, rather, confine these ritualistic mumblings of remembered excitements to a basic indication of warp and woof, trusting that, in tracing the final scheme of my tapestry, I do not become strangled, as it were, in the very weave and figure of our friends' horrid predicaments. An intertwining of the imbalances, both real and pretended, of our male unfortunates and their mates was, it quickly occurred to me, the very foundation of what continually shone out for me as our *conspiracy.* Edith, I perceived, to get on with it before the tangled web quite confounds this small effort of reconstruction, should "see" her first husband, poor Gregory, at every turn and corner, although he is in no wise *there,* having, to be abrupt about it, long since, I make no bones about it, died. This apparition must take the form of a retaliation for that embarrassment of—let me come out with the very word—Kleenex, which was, au fond, quite all that I had to begin with. It was to be, then, the "appearances" of Gregory which should drive poor Blaker to seek the comfort of the good Longstreths' assistance, but Longstreth—the beauty of this little turn of plot quite took my breath away—should, for retaliatory purposes of his own, be in the very midst of a magnificent pretending himself, namely, that his wife, who was always present, was, to his mind and eye, *never there*! At this glittering point of involvement I concluded, naturally enough, from the artistic viewpoint, that Mrs. Longstreth must also play some wonderful trick upon him. Here I needed, on Longstreth's part, a small crotchet, maggot, or compulsion upon which Lydia Longstreth could play her own little game of alarm and enlargement.

This compulsive act finally took the form for me of Longstreth's placing the wastebasket in the bathtub each night before going to bed, or, indeed, each evening before venturing out of the house for any purpose whatever. This simple gesture, called forth by the not unusual fear that wastebaskets may catch fire and consume one's house, is not in itself alarming in any profound sense, and it remained for me to transfigure it, as who should say. His wife, then, because of her own pretended failing grasp of the structures of immediacy

JAMES THURBER

must be painstakingly developed into a woman who no longer cares, to put it brutally, whether the house burns down or not. In point of fact, it may be her latent purpose to accomplish this very end, a proposition which at once illuminates, as by a show of searchlights, the loss of her own belief in poor Longstreth's significance as sanctuary. This, in its turn, would further and wonderfully sharpen our sense of poor Blaker's lostness when, at the farthest end, he calls so desperately upon his old guide and mentor for spiritual sustenance and emotional rehabilitation. Lydia Longstreth, I decided, should persuade her husband to put into the bathtub, not the wastebasket to which he was in the habit of tossing carelessly extinguished cigarets, but a brand-new metal receptacle which should be kept in the bathroom, all empty, for this one and only purpose. The meaninglessness of the compulsive act would thereby assume the proportions of the extremest futility and, I need scarcely belabor the point, inevitably result, if not in the burning down of the house, most surely in the collapse of minds and marriage, the effect of which upon Blaker should be, of course, staggering.

Whether Longstreth or Mrs. Longstreth, or both, even in these treacherous years of uncertain balance, could conceivably be "thrown" by the empty receptacle, whether it was, in short, *enough,* formed a dilemma of long concern to me, but I steadfastly refrained from, I sternly straight-armed, the temptation to introduce a psychiatrist into our little muddle, which was already losing lucidity with sufficient celerity. The temptation lay, I do admit it, in the frolic urge, common to most authors of our time, to bring in an authority on the psyche for the impish purpose of taking him "apart." This disassembling was to be signalled by the professional gentleman's distraught suggestion that the estranging couple should "put both baskets in the bathtub," but I hasten to repeat that some inner check dissuaded me from this extra and alien convolution. I take it as a matter of statistical truth that for every psychiatrist who "comes apart" there are, at a rough hazard, at least a hundred who mentally survive their patients, and this I regard as the happiest of circumstances. Moreover, I recommend the certainty of the small statistic to my more facetious colleagues in search of comic characters.

I needed, at this far point of ravelling and unravelling, a final twist of the threads of posture and imposture, to which I was inspired, by some dynamics of insight whose process now completely evades my

memory. It consisted, however, in the delightful notion that Longstreth, in greeting his old friend John Blaker on the latter's final visit,
is wearing, for all the warmth and coziness of the Longstreth drawing
room, not one hat, but, to get his wife "down"—I throw it out
vulgarly—and quite coincidentally to drive his frightened old friend
away from his door forever, *two*. But I shall leave our poor lost
conspirators at this gleaming point, lest these prefatory reminiscences
fairly outreach in area my little novella itself.

"The Old Friends" was of 1950, a year exceeded in acts and
moods of desperation, bewilderment, and despair only by the years
which had gone before and those which, God save us all, were still
to follow. I am not, at the longest of lasts, all unaware of the suspicion
which has fallen upon me, the suspicion that, in working out my
design, I have shown myself to be, in point of purpose, un-American.
It is of ancient record that I was, in fact, born in the States, but of
record almost as ancient that I duly became a resident and a national
of England, which plainly makes me and my small trade, if un-
anything, un-British, and there you may, my poor dear readers, in
whatever, spirit, leave me.

JAMES THURBER

Belles Lettres and Me

THURBER AT LARGE IN THE WRITERS' COMMUNITY

"There isn't room in this house for belles lettres and me both."

The Harpers and Their Circle

(After reading Margaret Case Harriman's *The Vicious Circle,* a fond history of the wits, male and female, who used to gather at the famous Round Table in the Algonquin Hotel in New York.)

The original firm of Harper & Brothers, founded more than 100 years ago, consisted of five brothers who took turns being Harper. Whenever an irate author stormed into the office demanding to see Harper, whatever brother he accosted would say simply, "Harper is out" or "Harper is not in." It was Charles Dickens, on one of his visits to America, who gave the firm its first example of authorial wrath. He opposed strenuously, for some reason, the intention of Harper & Brothers to bring out his famous novel under the title of "Oliver H. P. Twist," which they held to be smarter than plain Oliver Twist.

One of the brothers, possibly the current Harper, had the notion, during the firm's first year, of interviewing authors, not in the editorial offices, but at the now famous Long Table in the old (then, to be sure, the new) Fifth Avenue Hotel. The luncheons held there, almost daily for sixty-five years, were expensive and took up a great deal of time, but the practice turned out to be worthwhile, since the complex authors rarely put on distressing scenes in the staid and dignified dining-room. There was, of course, some trouble with Edgar Allan Poe every few weeks, but the fault was almost always someone else's, not Poe's. One noon, for example, a pretty young woman, a total stranger to Poe and to the others at the table, ran up to the famous poet and short-story writer, flung her arms about his neck, kissed him on the cheek, and cried, "Ah simply adore 'The Goldberg.' " Poe gave the fair intruder his pensive smile and said, "Madam, you must be thinking of 'Love Among the Ryans.' " The young lady, far from being taken aback, turned coolly to the others at the table, Harper and his brothers, Robert Browning and his wife, Elizabeth Barrett Browning, Nat Hawthorne, Jimmy Fenimore Cooper and Herman ("Mank") Melville, and said, "Mah name is Ann Brothers, an Ah simply adore all of you men!" Poe gave her his darkest look and said, "Screw loose and fancy free." It was Melville who announced, before any of the others had figured it out, "This young lady is a natural for our group, and I propose that we think of her, from now on, as Harper Ann Brothers."

Miss Brothers said she was from the deep South, but Poe didn't believe it. "Butter wouldn't melt in your South," he said.

The passages at arms between the poet and the girl reached their highest point one day in the summer of 1858, when Poe asked her if she had ever been to school. "Yes," said Miss Brothers, who had apparently been waiting for this question for several years, "but I liked philosophers better than poets. You see, I put Descartes before Horace." This kind of wit was vehemently objected to by the Tablers on the ground that it was synthetic and planned, or, as we would say today, "rigged."

"Merciful God," moaned Poe, "what have I ever done to deserve this?" "Haven't the critics told you?" Miss Brothers asked sweetly, setting the table aroar.

Jimmy Cooper and Poe never got along very well, possibly because Cooper always called the author of "Ulalume" by the name of "Edmund." There had also been the tense moment when Cooper interrupted Poe's babbling to say, "Your Lenore isn't lost. She's hiding." When Cooper's *The Deerslayer* was published, and he came late to the table that day, wreathed in smiles, Poe referred to him as "the Merchant of Venison." Everybody laughed except Browning, who held Poe's wit in low esteem, and when the merriment had died down, the author of *The Ring and the Book* said, "Edgar thinks he is the man who put the laughter in 'slaughter,' whereas, as a matter of fact, he is the man who took it out, leaving only a faint hissing sound." This was too much for Poe, who could not think offhand of a sharp retort, and he contented himself with the nasty assertion, "Browning, all your poems are at least eight hundred lines too long." Browning flashed his pensive smile. "As against your sonnets, sir," he said, "which are never more than fourteen lines too long." A lively, but edged argument then arose about the relative merits of various poets, including Longfellow, to whom Poe always alluded as "Henry Wordsworth," and presently, Browning lost his temper and said to Poe, "You do not know the half of poetry." Poe was ready for this one. "Poe *is* the half of poetry," he pointed out quietly, and Browning, God bless him, was ready for *that* one. "Yes, I know that," he said sweetly, "but the other half is 'try,' something you have never successfully done." When the merriment had died down, Elizabeth Barrett Browning was gone, nobody knew where.

Ralph Waldo Emerson was asked to the Long Table once, and then never again. Some of the other Americans who frequented the celebrated dining room were jealous of his trips to Europe and of his friendship with Thomas Carlyle. Poe, for some reason, did not admire the English historian's writings, which he considered full of sound and fury. Poe once called him, in Emerson's presence, "Tom Tom Carlyle," and this enraged the Concord philosopher. Furthermore, it was generally believed that Carlyle affected glasses with green lenses, which caused Poe to remark, unfairly, "Tom Tom is the green-eyed punster." On the occasion of poor Emerson's one and only harried luncheon in the famous dining-room, Poe kept insisting that the author of "English Traits" had been a Rhodes scholar. "I am not a Rhodes scholar, and I have never been one," Emerson said testily. Poe gave him his pensive smile. "I know that, Waldo," he said, "but you look at life through Rhodes-scholared glasses." This over-elaborate and clearly rigged retort was considered out of bounds, and Melville got up and left the table, along with Emerson. The former came back, but the latter never did.

Speaking of leaving the table, there was the day Poe thought he had, when he actually hadn't. At this luncheon, Charlotte Brontë was present, and Harper, for her amusement, pretended to have had too much wine, since this was necessary to get off his little gag. The brothers scarcely ranked with their famous authors as wits, and usually merely applauded a jape or a quip lightly, or exclaimed softly, "Jolly, Oh!" or "Oh, Jolly!", but now and again they liked to have their innings. "How many Brontës are there?" Harper asked the author of *Wuthering Heights* that day. "There are three of us," she said. This was what Harper was waiting for. "Yes," he said, "and I can see all three of you." Miss Brontë was not to be outdone, however. "We," she said sweetly, "can see all three of you, too." It was at this point that Poe thought he left the table. As a matter of fact, it was one of the Harpers who got up and went back to the office. For more than an hour, Poe, believing he was absent, did not touch his drink. "Do you know something, Edgar?" Harper asked suddenly, and the surprised poet said, "Why don't you ask me some day when I'm here?" Harper was taken aback and said, "But you are here, Edgar!" Poe favored him with his darkest gaze, "Dammit, sir," he said, "I was having such a good time listening to myself being talked about behind my back." This time there was no merriment to die down, because none of the Harpers got the point of Poe's remark, and Miss Brontë, it turned out, had not been listening.

In my next chapter, if any, I will tell about the amusing, and sometimes disastrous, situations that arose during the ten years that the charter members of the Long Table were joined at their luncheons by Henry George and Henry James. Their continual presence bothered Poe, who found it difficult to tell one of the men from the other, and there were long months when he stayed away. To Ann Brothers, however, it was easy to make a distinction between the author of *The Ambassadors* and the author of *Progress and Poverty*. One day, just before Poe left the table, to be gone all summer, she said sweetly, "Ah cain't unnahstand whah you all cain't tell Mistah Joge from Mistah James. One is the single tax man, and the other is the syntax man." This time, when Poe got up and left the table, he knew he was no longer there.

A Visit from Saint Nicholas

(IN THE ERNEST HEMINGWAY MANNER)

It was the night before Christmas. The house was very quiet. No creatures were stirring in the house. There weren't even any mice stirring. The stockings had been hung carefully by the chimney. The children hoped that Saint Nicholas would come and fill them.

The children were in their beds. Their beds were in the room next to ours. Mamma and I were in our beds. Mamma wore a kerchief. I had my cap on. I could hear the children moving. We didn't move. We wanted the children to think we were asleep.

"Father," the children said.

There was no answer. He's there, all right, they thought.

"Father," they said, and banged on their beds.

"What do you want?" I asked.

"We have visions of sugarplums," the children said.

"Go to sleep," said mamma.

"We can't sleep," said the children. They stopped talking, but I could hear them moving. They made sounds.

"Can you sleep?" asked the children.

"No," I said.

"You ought to sleep."

"I know. I ought to sleep."

"Can we have some sugarplums?"

"You can't have any sugarplums," said mamma.

"We just asked you."

There was a long silence. I could hear the children moving again.

JAMES THURBER

"Is Saint Nicholas asleep?" asked the children.

"No," mamma said. "Be quiet."

"What the hell would he be asleep tonight for?" I asked.

"He might be," the children said.

"He isn't," I said.

"Let's try to sleep," said mamma.

The house became quiet once more. I could hear the rustling noises the children made when they moved in their beds.

Out on the lawn a clatter arose. I got out of bed and went to the window. I opened the shutters; then I threw up the sash. The moon shone on the snow. The moon gave the lustre of mid-day to objects in the snow. There was a miniature sleigh in the snow, and eight tiny reindeer. A little man was driving them. He was lively and quick. He whistled and shouted at the reindeer and called them by their names. Their names were Dasher, Dancer, Prancer, Vixen, Comet, Cupid, Donder, and Blitzen.

He told them to dash away to the top of the porch, and then he told them to dash away to the top of the wall. They did. The sleigh was full of toys.

"Who is it?" mamma asked.

"Some guy," I said. "A little guy."

I pulled my head in out of the window and listened. I heard the reindeer on the roof. I could hear their hoofs pawing and prancing on the roof. "Shut the window," said mamma. I stood still and listened.

"Reindeer," I said. I shut the window and walked about. It was cold. Mamma sat up in the bed and looked at me.

"How would they get on the roof?" mamma asked.

"They fly."

"Get into bed. You'll catch cold."

Mamma lay down in bed. I didn't get into bed. I kept walking around.

"What do you mean, they fly?" asked mamma.

"Just fly is all."

Mamma turned away toward the wall. She didn't say anything.

I went out into the room where the chimney was. The little man came down the chimney and stepped into the room. He was dressed all in fur. His clothes were covered with ashes and soot from the chimney. On his back was a pack like a peddler's pack. There were toys in it. His cheeks and nose were red and he had dimples. His eyes twinkled. His mouth was little, like a bow, and his beard was very white. Between his teeth was a stumpy pipe. The smoke from the pipe encircled his head in a wreath. He laughed and his belly shook. It shook like a bowl of red jelly. I laughed. He winked his eye, then he gave a twist to his head. He didn't say anything.

He turned to the chimney and filled the stockings and turned away from the chimney. Laying his fingers aside his nose, he gave a nod. Then he went up the chimney and looked up. I saw him get into his sleigh. He whistled at his team and the team flew away. The team flew as lightly as thistledown. The driver called out, "Merry Christmas and good night." I went back to bed.

"What was it?" asked mamma. "Saint Nicholas?" She smiled.

"Yeah," I said.

She sighed and turned in the bed.

"I saw him," I said.

"Sure."

"I did see him."

"Sure you saw him." She turned farther toward the wall.

"Father," said the children.

"There you go," mamma said. "You and your flying reindeer."

"Go to sleep," I said.

"Can we see Saint Nicholas when he comes?" the children asked.

"You got to be asleep," I said. "You got to be asleep when he comes. You can't see him unless you're unconscious."

"Father knows," mamma said.

I pulled the covers over my mouth. It was warm under the covers. As I went to sleep I wondered if mamma was right.

JAMES THURBER

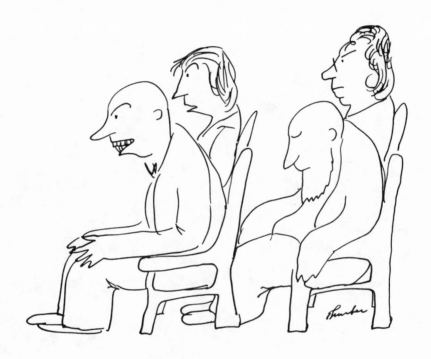

Ravel's "Bolero."

Folks out of Faulkner.

An Evening with Carl Sandburg

EDITOR'S NOTE: Thurber met "the singing poet" Carl Sandburg while both were visiting Columbus, Thanksgiving of 1936. After Sandburg's concert, at a friend's reception, Thurber and Sandburg carried on rather exclusively. Thurber admired and was admired by Sandburg and recounted the festive evening in drawings and an accompanying letter (not included here).

Dance Recital.

JAMES THURBER

Sandburg Tells a Story.

Jeez, it <u>looks</u> like Sandburg's plane, don't it?

COLLECTING HIMSELF

No More Biographies

I dropped around to see Rumsonby at his office in the Congressional Library at Washington. Rumsonby had charge of the Bureau of Publishing Statistics and Biographers' Permits, which had been created by act of Congress in 1940, shortly after seven different lives of Harding and twenty-eight different biographies of Lincoln came out in one day. I had been away from the country for a great many years, and I didn't really know what was going on in the book-publishing world. Rumsonby, I knew, would make it all clear to me.

"Hello," he said. "I hope you don't want a permit to do a biography, especially of a Civil War character. All I got left in that line is Captain Charles O. Schultz of the Sixty-seventh Ohio Volunteer Infantry. All the other officers have passed their quota."

"You mean a biography has been written about every officer who was in the Civil War except this Schultz?" I asked.

"*A* biography?" he echoed. "There were ninety-two Lees and ninety-five Grants when the law went into effect. The books on Lincoln alone ran to forty million copies. Something had to be done. A government statistician discovered that if all the biographies in America were laid end to end, they would cover the entire surface of the United States, ten times over. That means that if people started laying their biographies end to end outdoors, we would all be bogged in books up to our knees. Traffic would stop, production and distribution of foodstuffs would be handicapped, army maneuvers would—"

EDITOR'S NOTE: The year of publication, 1932, is key for reading this reprint with its intended parody since the 1940 act of Congress to which Thurber refers is in the future for its original reader.

JAMES THURBER

118

"But the people aren't going to lay their books end to end out-doors," I said.

"They might," said Rumsonby. "Anyway, there had to be a federal regulation, if only to conserve house space. Long ago as 1935, as many as eighty-four books a day were being published, with an average sale of a thousand copies. That meant that about twenty-five million volumes a year were flooding the country. Or two hundred and fifty-two million in ten years. The total shelf space, counting pantries, in the United States is only—"

"It would have been interesting to let it go on at that rate and see what would happen," I said.

"We knew what would happen," said Rumsonby. "It would have meant a disastrous decline in the purchase of furniture, woollens, foodstuffs, and so on, in order to make room in the house for books. Eventually a war of aggression and conquest would have been necessary to get space for all the books."

Rumsonby began writing down a lot of big numbers on a sheet of paper, apparently trying to figure out how large a country we'd have had to conquer to get room for the books.

"Supposing," I said, "I published a volume on Grant, or Jeb Stuart, or Stonewall Jackson tomorrow?"

Rumsonby referred to a little book at his elbow.

"Let's see," he said. "The fine for Grant is five thousand dollars, for Stuart thirty-two hundred and fifty, and for Jackson four thousand. Your books would be confiscated too, of course."

"How about Lincoln?" I asked.

"Lincoln carries a maximum fine of fifty thousand dollars and two years' imprisonment or both. Everybody wants to do Lincoln. There was the famous case of one biographer who got around the letter of the law by writing a volume on Lincoln which was fictive and supposi-tional. It was called "If Lincoln Had Shot Booth." The Supreme Court decided that the author was not guilty of breaking the law because his book was not biography in the technical sense of the word; that is, it was not an actual account of a person's life. This opinion led to seventy-four other If books on Lincoln, including "If Lincoln Had Missed Booth," "If Booth Had Hit Mrs. Lincoln," "If Mrs. Lincoln Had Shot Mrs. Booth," and so on. It was terribly confusing. Eventually schoolchildren got the idea that Lincoln was alive and that the South had won. An amendment to the biography law was passed prohibiting the writing of imaginary biographies of persons whose quotas had been passed."

"I suppose," I said, "that the quota has been reached in the case of Henry VIII, Elizabeth, and the prominent American financiers, such as Rockefeller, Morgan, etc."

"It would cost you five hundred dollars to publish a book on any royal Englishman, dead or alive," said Rumsonby. "As for American men of business, the only one who hasn't had a biography written about him is Herbert S. Kingsley, president of the Eighth Avenue Bank of Ogdensburg, New York. You want him?"

"No," I said.

"Somebody'll pick up him before the week's out," said Rumsonby. The phone on his desk rang and he took up the receiver. "Bureau for the Prohibition of Biographies," he said, in a singsong voice. "Who? Lieutenant-Colonel George Babcock? Wait a minute. Hold on now. Is that Lieutenant-Colonel George Babcock of the Thirty-first Mississippi? Sorry, he's been done. By a Mrs. Ann Meadows, of St. Martin's Parish, Louisiana." Rumsonby hung up.

"Is anything being done to stop the glut of novels?" I asked.

"There's some talk," said my friend, "of a federal statute restricting novels about little groups of people going to pieces through drinking and carousing around with each other's mates. Geographical allocation of such groups has been suggested as the best means of regulation. For instance, since 1932 there have been upwards of four thousand novels dealing with groups of people going to pieces in Long Island, Manhattan, and the Riviera alone. They'd have to do it somewhere else, with a limit on the number of books to a given region."

"Sounds like something Congress would enjoy," I said. "Now, listen. Suppose a character in a novel suddenly began telling the life of Lincoln and told it all?"

"There's a case like that up before the Supreme Court now," said Rumsonby. "Fellow has brought out a book in which a little group of people go to pieces in Miami, Florida, and one of them, at a wild party, tells a new life of General P. G. T. Beauregard. The penalty for a life of Beauregard is sixteen hundred dollars and sixty days' imprisonment or both. It's up to the Supreme Court."

JAMES THURBER

How to Tell
a Fine Old Wine

In spite of all that has been written about wines, the confusion in the minds of some lay drinkers is just as foggy as it was—in the case of some minds, even foggier. The main trouble, I think, is that the average wine connoisseur has suddenly become rather more the writing man than the sipping man without possessing that fine precision in expository composition which comes only from long years of writing, rewriting, cutting down, and, most especially, throwing away. It is my hope in this article, somehow or other, to clear up a few of the more involved problems of nomenclature and of geographical (or viticultural) distribution, for I believe I know what the wine experts have been trying to say and I believe I can say it perhaps a little more clearly.

France, then, is divided into ninety different *Départements,* all but four of them ending in *"et-Oise"* (and-Oise) and twenty-seven of them having towns named Châlons. Fortunately, in only three of the Châlons *communes* are there *girondes* where any of the great wines of France are grown. We can safely confine ourselves to the Bordeaux region and the Burgundy region, respectively the *Côte-d'Or* and the *Côte de Châlons,* or as the French trainmen say, *"L'autre côté!"* The great wines of France are divided into only three classifications with which we need to be concerned: the *grands vins,* the *petits vins,* and the *vins fins.* And it is with the last that we shall be most particularly concerned. *Vins fins* means, simply enough, "finished wines," that is, wines which did not turn out as well as might have been expected.

JAMES THURBER

It is these wines and none others which America is getting today and which America is going to continue to get. Just what causes this I don't exactly know, but something.

In the old days of the great *châteauxiers,* there was never any question about what to do with a *vin* when it turned out to be *fin.* The *châteauxiers* simply referred to it philosophically as *"fin de siècle"* (finished for good) and threw it out. They would have nothing to do with a wine that wasn't noble, distinguished, dignified, courageous, high-souled, and austere. Nowadays it is different. The *vins fins* are filtered through to the American public in a thousand different disguises, all spurious—not a genuine disguise among them. It is virtually impossible for the layman, when he picks up a bottle labelled "St. Julien-Clos Vougeot-Grandes Veuves, 1465A21, *mise du château,* Perdolio, Premier Cru, Marchanderie: Carton et Cie., 1924," to know whether he is getting, as should be the case with this label, a truly noble St. Estèphe or, as is more likely to be the case, a Benicarló that has been blended with Heaven only knows what, perhaps even a white Margelaise! Well then, how *is* he to know?

Let us say that a bottle has come into our hands labelled as above. "St. Julien" is simply the name of the *commune* and "Clos Vougeot" the name of the château around which the grapes are grown. "Grandes Veuves" is either an added distinguishing flourish put on the noble old label years and years ago by some *grandes veuves* (large widows) or it is a meaningless addition placed thereon since repeal by those French *flâneurs* who hope to inveigle the American public into buying cheap and tawdry wines under elaborate and impressive-sounding labels. So much for the name of the wine itself.

The number, 1465A21, is nothing to be bewildered by. It is simply the official *estampe française de la douane* and it can be checked against the authentic "serial-running" of the official French revenue stamping machine by applying to somebody in the French Embassy here, or the French Consulate, and asking him to get in touch with the man in charge of the registered files of the French revenue stamping department. If the letter used (in this case "A") proves to be the actual letter employed in 1924 by the revenue stampers, the vintage date on the bottle is authentic, providing, of course, that the identifying letter was, in that year, inserted between the fourth and fifth figures of the serial number and that 146521 fell among the *estampages* allocated to the St. Julien *commune* in that year. It is, of course, unfortunate that the Stavisky affair in France threw all the numbers in that country into the wildest sort of confusion, so that it is hardly likely that any stamp numbers can be certified with confidence by anybody for the next six months or so. But the wine will be all the better after six months and France may by then have its records in order once more, if she can find them.

The phrase *"mise du château"* is extremely simple, and it is astonishing how many Americans are puzzled by it. It means nothing more than "mice in the château," just as it says. The expression goes back to the days, some twenty years ago, when certain French manufacturers of popular "tonic wines" made fortunes almost overnight and in many cases bought up old châteaux, tore them down, and built lavish new ones in the rococo manner. These new châteaux were, of course, clean and well kept, but so garish and ugly that a disdainful expression grew up among the French peasantry in regard to them: *"Ils n'ont jamais de mise du château là-bas"* ("They never have any mice in that château over there"). The grand old *châteauxiers* thereupon began to add to their labels, *"mise du château"*—in other words, "There are mice in *this* château," a proud if slightly incongruous legend for a bottle of noble old wine.

The label symbol "Perdolio" on our bottle might equally well have been "Manfreda," "Variola," "Muscatel," "Amontillado," "Sauternes," "Katerina," or any one of a couple of hundred others. The idea of this name originated with the old Spanish *vinteriosos,* especially those of Casanovia and Valencia, and indicated simply a desire on the part of a given merchant to place the name of a favorite daughter, son, mistress, or wine on the bottles he merchandised.

"Premier Cru," which we come to next in looking back at our St. Julien label, means "first growth," that is, wine that was grown first. And "Marchanderie: Carton et Cie." is the name of the shipper. In some cases the name of the captain of the ship transporting the wine is also added to the label, some such name as Graves or Médoc, and one need not take alarm at this, but one should be instantly suspicious of any marks, names, numbers, or symbols other than those I have gone into here. Bottles which bear such legends as "George H., Kansas City, '24" or "C. M. & Bessie B., '18" or "Mrs. P. P. Bliss, Ashtabula, O., '84" or "I Love My Wife But Oh You Kid (1908)" may be put down as having fallen into the hands of American tourists

JAMES THURBER

somewhere between the bottling and the shipping. They are doubtlessly refills containing a colored sugar water, if anything at all.

The vintage year is, of course, always branded into the cork of the bottle and is the only kind of bottle-cork date mark to go by. Dates laid in with mother-of-pearl or anything of the sort are simply impressive and invidious attempts to force high prices from the pockets of gullible Americans. So also are French wine labels bearing the American flag or portraits of Washington or such inscriptions, no matter how beautifully engraved or colored, as "Columbia, the Gem of the Ocean" and "When Lilacs Last in the Dooryard Grew."

In summing up, it is perhaps advisable to say a few words about the vineyards themselves. Some vineyards, facing north, get the morning sun just under the right side of the leaf; others, facing south, get the sun on the other side. Many vineyards slope and many others do not. Once in a while one straggles into a graveyard or climbs up on a porch. In each case a difference may or may not be found in the quality of the wine. When a town has been built on the place where a vineyard formerly was, the vineyard is what the French call "out" (a word adopted from our English tennis term). There may be a few vines still producing in gutters and backyards of the town, but the quality of their output will be ignoble. The "out" taste is easily discernible to both the connoisseur and the layman just as is the faint flavor of saddle polish in certain brands of sparkling Burgundy. In the main, it is safe to go by one's taste. Don't let anybody tell you it is one-tenth as hard to tell the taste of a good wine from the taste of a bad wine or even of a so-so wine as some of the *connaisseurs écrivants* would have us believe.

What Price a Farewell
to Designs?

Ten years ago, when I was just a little shaver (shaving every other day, instead of simply letting the whole thing go, as I do now), almost every other article that appeared in any periodical you might pick up, from the *New York Times Sunday Magazine* to *Gentlemen's Needlework*, was entitled What Price This or What Price That: "What Price Peace?" "What Price Farm Relief?" "What Price Naval Oil Reserves?" "What Price Prohibition in Norway?" "What Price Preservation of President Monroe's Old Prince Street House?" "What Price U.S. Senator Grisbaum, the Man and the Public Servant?"

This went on for several years. Then came the "A Farewell to" epoch: "A Farewell to Prosperity," "A Farewell to Religion," "A Farewell to Happiness," "A Farewell to Romance," "A Farewell to Love," "A Farewell to Peace," "A Farewell to Security," "A Farewell to Loyalty," "A Farewell to Honor," "A Farewell to Happy Days," "A Farewell to President Monroe's Old Prince Street House," "A Farewell to Senator Grisbaum, the Man and the Public Servant." (During this melancholy period there was some slight vogue for "A Preface to" titles, but this never really took hold for the reason that people were much more interested in kissing things goodbye than in being introduced to things.)

This went on for several years. Then, this winter, came (and if it were a snake, it would bite you) the "Design for" era. This will go on for several years: "Design for Leaving," "Design for Loving," "Design for Luring," "Design for Laughing," "Design for Lifting,"

JAMES THURBER

"Design for Lowering," "Design for Lying," "Design for Looping," "Design for Loafing," "Design for Loping," "Design for Leaping," "Design for Limping," "Design for Preserving President Monroe's Old Prince Street House," etc.

Each of these title patterns could be shown to express the public temper of its time. A graph, indeed, could be worked out representing the mental attitude of the nation during the periods involved, but it would probably be left lying around and get thrown out by the cook. Suffice it, then, simply to point out that in the "What Price" days people were interested in what was going to come of everything; in the "Farewell to" days, they were apathetic about what became of anything; in the present "Design for" days, they are evincing a slight revival of interest in planning for the future. This set of conclusions, admittedly specious, is not, however, the main point I wish to make. What has interested me mostly in my researches (which involved going back over the files of everything, from 1880 to 1923) is that I found no title patterns at all comparable to the "What Price," "A Farewell to," and "Design for" phenomena. The only conclusion I could come to is that, although there were popular and famous titles of books and plays in the old days, they didn't seem to lend themselves to paraphrase. Take, for example, "Beside the Bonny Brier Bush." An article on the strategy of Lord Nelson could hardly have been entitled "Beside the Bonny Strategy of Lord Nelson." It would have lacked ease. The same problem seems to have come up in the case of Clyde Fitch's well-known play, "The Girl with the Green Eyes." I encountered an article, printed at the time of that play's popularity, called "Rabbit Trapping in the Western Reserve." There had apparently been no effort to call it "The Girl with Rabbit Trapping in the Western Reserve" (although, of course, there was no way of being *sure* that there hadn't been some effort). Similarly, "Little Lord Fauntleroy" failed to leave its imprint on the pages of forgotten periodicals; there was no "Little Lord Tariff Problems of Today," no "Little Lord Alarming Increase of Scorching on the Public Highways." This unadaptability held true also for "The Memoirs of U.S. Grant," "Sherlock Holmes," "Secret Service," "Captain Jinks of the Horse Marines" (a specially notable instance), "Lucile," "The Squaw Man," etc.

I did not, it is only fair to admit, check *all* titles of books and plays with *all* titles of articles in the years between 1880 and 1923. If I had, this would have been a comprehensive and important article, maybe even a standard source article. The trouble was that I got to a point in my researches where I not only forgot what I was trying to prove but also what I was looking up. As a result, I spent one whole afternoon at the Public Library clipping pictures of navy officers and show girls out of back copies of *Munsey's*. They do not fit anywhere into my design for grieving over a farewell to old-fashioned titles. But I found one swell Dewey.

JAMES THURBER

The Literary Meet

The ladies' literary society has come under the influence of the magazine *Liberty,* which has set a new vogue in Belles Lettres by announcing, before each article, the official reading time—for example: 14 minutes, 30 seconds. The gathering of the Wednesday Afternoon Browning Club is therefore known as a Meet, instead of a meeting. It was run off this week at the home of Mrs. Charles F. Turnbush, and was won by the Blues with a total point score of 36 1/2. The Red ladies finished with but 11 1/2. Previous to the matches, Mrs. Carl Dittledorf gave an exhibition against time, clipping 32 seconds off par for "Bishop Blougram's Apology."

The sprints this week were particularly interesting. W. E. Henley's "Invictus" was won by Mrs. George Preen, of 247 Civic Park Drive, in 8 2/5 seconds, lowering by two-fifths of a second the previous mark, set two weeks ago by Mrs. Harry Leeper, of The Elms, Glenn Junction. Poe's "To Helen" was also won by Mrs. Preen in the snappy time of 6 1/5 seconds, tying her own previous record of the second meet in August.

In the middle distances, the "Evangeline" of Longfellow was a particularly stirring event. It was won by Mrs. Katherine Murch, a house guest of Mrs. Turnbush, in 30 minutes and 26 seconds. This is a new world's record. Mrs. Leeper, who finished in 30 minutes and 18 seconds, was disqualified for slurring her nouns.

The long-distance match this week was the reading of the *New York Times* editorial page for September 18. It was won by Mrs. Goldie Trinkham, the mother of two lovely children, in 1 hour, 14 minutes, and 7 seconds. Mrs. Preen, despite her fine work in the sprints, entered this competition also, but was forced to drop out at the bottom of the second column. Mrs. Emma Giles, who led until the middle of the third column, was lapped when she went back and re-read a paragraph to get the sense of an editorial on the French budget.

The feature of the meet was "Twinkle, Twinkle, Little Star," for the kiddies. Little Gretta Preen won this event in the time of 2 3/5 seconds. Little Miss Genevieve Leeper was disqualified for leaving out one twinkle. The ladies of the club are all giving one hour a day to literary work, this consisting largely of deep breathing exercises and other methods of increasing their reading scope.

JAMES THURBER

"How is it possible, woman, in the awful and magnificent times we live in, to be preoccupied exclusively with the piddling?"

"I want to send that one about 'Instead of hearts and cupid's darts I'm sending you a wire,' or whatever the hell it is!"

"The trouble is you make me think too much."

"Well, I call it Caribbean, and I intend to go to my grave calling it Caribbean."

JAMES THURBER

"Hey, Joe. How d'ya spell 'rhythm'?"

Memoirs of a
Banquet Speaker

The sanity of the average banquet speaker lasts about two and a half months; at the end of that time he begins to mutter to himself, and calls out in his sleep. I am dealing here with the young banquet speaker, the dilettante, who goes into it in quest of glamour. There is, he finds out too late, no glamour at banquets—I mean the large formal banquets of big associations and societies. There is only a kind of dignified confusion that gradually unhinges the mind.

Late in my thirty-fifth year, having tasted every other experience in life (except being rescued by Captain Fried), I decided to be a guest of honor at some glittering annual dinner in a big New York hotel. At first blush, you might think it would be difficult to be asked. It isn't. You don't, of course, have to be a member of an organization in order to address its annual banquet. In fact the organization doesn't even have to know who you are, and it almost never does. The names of the speakers are got out of newspapers and phone books, and from the better Christmas cards; sometimes a speaker is suggested to the entertainment committee by a woman named Mrs. Grace Voynton. That's all I know about her. She suggested me. I never saw her again. As a matter of fact, I never saw her at all. She phoned me one day and asked if I would address the annual banquet of a certain organization, the name of which, in the ensuing conversation, which was rather controversial, slipped my mind. I said I wouldn't address the banquet because my dinner pants were too tight. She was pleased to regard this as a pleasantry, and phoned me again the next day, as a woman will. Finally I said I would make a short talk. I was told to be at the Commodore Hotel at seven-thirty on a certain Wednesday evening. It was only when I was in a taxi on my way to the hotel that I realized I didn't know the name, or the nature, of the organization I was going to talk to—let alone what I was going to talk about. So high is the courage of youth that the young banquet speaker is likely to dismiss this unfortunate ignorance too lightly. He has an idea that Mrs. Voynton will be at the hotel, or that the doorman will recognize him. Certainly, he thinks, it is going to be easy enough to find the banquet-room. It *isn't* going to be, though (the italics are mine). During the banqueting season anywhere from three to eleven banquets are being held, simultaneously, at the average hotel on any given night. Not realizing this, the young guest of honor is almost sure to think that the first banquet table he spies is the one at which he belongs. There is only about one chance in ten that he is right.

I walked into the first banquet-room that I came to, on the mezzanine floor, after having been met by no one at all except a man who asked me where the ladies' dressing-room was. I told him I didn't know and he walked over and told a lady who was with him that I didn't know. There is no reason in the world why a trivial incident like that should unnerve a banquet speaker; it leaves him, however, with a vague sense of insecurity: he begins to wonder where he is, and what night it is, and whether the whole thing may not possibly be a hoax.

In somewhat of a daze—the first warning of a bad mental state—I found myself seated at a long table on a dais, next to a lady who asked me, as soon as I had drunk a glass of ice water, if I understood the makeup and purposes of the organization we were about to address. She had also accepted over the phone, and had had a miserable connection. I told her facetiously—as one who whistles in the dark to keep his nerve up—that I was under the impression we were the guests of honor at the National Women's Bulb-Raising Association. This caused the man on her right to pale slightly. He drank a little water and whispered to me that, on the contrary, we were at the annual dinner of the North-Eastern States Meat-Handlers Association. I could see, however, that he was uncertain of himself on that point: he kept twisting his napkin. After the coffee and ice cream he was called upon for the first speech of the evening, and if ever a man touched lightly on the meat-handling situation he did. His nervous condition and incoherent remarks obviously upset the toastmaster who, all we speakers were instantly aware, was not absolutely sure that he was at the right banquet himself.

At this point, since I figured that several speakers were yet to come before I would be called on, I slipped from the table and made a hasty trip to the lobby to look up the sign which tells where the various conventions are being held. Several were listed, and their locations were given merely as Ballroom A, Ballroom B, Second Assembly Hall, Jade Room, etc. It was impossible to identify these rooms in the short time at my disposal and so I simply hurried back to my seat. From the sign, however, I had discovered that there was a possibility I might be in the midst of the National Chassis-Builders Association, the Society for the Advancement of Electric Welding, the American Society of Syrup and Fondant Makers, or the Past Presidents and Active Officers of Ye Olde Record Binding Company.

As I sat in my chair, breathing heavily, I tried to think up a few words of greeting and appreciation which might apply equally to the aims and purposes of all the various organizations. This got me nowhere at all. Nor did I receive any help from the gentleman who was talking at the moment. His expression was the agonized expression of a man who hasn't the slightest idea what it is all about and wishes he were home. He told four stories, in a husky voice, and sat down. The toastmaster now arose and said that we were going to have the pleasure of listening to a man who knew more about the subject nearest our hearts than anyone else in America, a man whose great authority in this field has been recognized by his being selected to write on the subject for the new *Encyclopaedia Britannica* (I quote him more or less accurately—it was a little more involved than that). Instead of naming his man at this juncture, the toastmaster told a story, and then reverted to the world's greatest authority on the subject nearest our hearts, repeating what he had already said, and finally, with a sweep of his hand, pronouncing the speaker's name— "Mr. Septimus R. Groves." As the toastmaster sat down, I lapsed back into my chair and applauded lightly. Nobody got up. All eyes then followed the toastmaster's—and rested finally on me. I knew now that I was at the wrong banquet. Vaguely, as I got to my feet, I wondered where Mr. Groves was, and on what subject he was so

JAMES THURBER

eminent an authority. I was received with tremendous applause. When it quieted down I began to speak. I sketched briefly the advance of transportation, the passing of riveting, the improvement shown in the handling and distribution of meats, chassis construction, electric welding, and the absolute reliance that one could place nowadays upon the binding of old records. In conclusion I left with my audience the thought that in meat-handling, as in bulb-raising, and binding old records, it is Service and Coöperation that count. The speech was received with thunderous applause and a little stomping.

It was not until I got into a taxi that I realized my mind was already beginning to go. The driver asked me where to. I was surprised to hear myself tell him the Pennsylvania Hotel. There I registered as "Septimus R. Groves." "We already have a Septimus R. Groves registered here," said the clerk, with polite interest. "What's his name?" I asked. "Septimus R. Groves," he said. "He's attending the annual banquet of the Fish and Game Wardens." "Oh," I said, "there must be some mistake; the man you're thinking of is Horace R. Morgner—gypsum blocks and building laths." The clerk gave me my room key, albeit with a certain reluctance. It was a week before I went home. I don't mutter any longer, but I still cry out in my sleep.

A Mile and a Half of Lines

THURBER ON HIS DRAWINGS

Answers-to-Hard-Questions Department

To the Editors of *The New Yorker*

Sirs:

Has *The New Yorker* got a policy on drawings, sketches, etc., as I draw rather easily and would like to submit some. I understand you want only sophisticated or smart pictures, and would like to know if this is correct, and who does the captions, the artist or the editors? Please explain your covers also.

Respectfully,
H—— C——

Dear H—— C——

All that *The New Yorker* has ever had in the shape of a written policy on drawings is a set of rules, for the guidance of the office staff, setting forth what must be done with drawings when they are received. In the early years of the magazine thousands of drawings got lost around the office and never were found. This set the artists crazy. As one of them, whose style had grown outmoded while he was trying to learn where his drawings had got to, said to us, "What the hell is the use of submitting pictures to you if you are going to become gradually unaware of where they are?" There was no satisfactory answer to that at the time—and still isn't. This situation, in the first year or two of *The New Yorker*'s life, led to friction, ill-feeling, and catcalling between the artists and the editors and, finally, in the famous case of the Charles Durande drawings, to a lawsuit. Durande was an artist who claimed he had sent six or eight hundred pictures to the magazine over a period of a year and a half, for which he received no money, which were never used, and which he never got back. The upshot was that the magazine had to pay Durande a hundred and eighty-seven thousand dollars for drawings which no one, except Mr. and Mrs. Durande and some friends of theirs, had ever seen, or, for the matter of that, ever will see. Because of annoying little incidents like that, a system of handling drawings finally had to be instituted. In the last year or two it has been working smoothly and no drawings have been lost, except a few of the smaller ones.

As to what kind of drawings *The New Yorker* wants, I find it difficult, even at this period of the magazine's development, to formulate a written policy which will make sense. All I can do is cite a few random instances of pictures that didn't work out, draw a few diagrams, and indicate roughly the field we are trying to cover. The diagrams are going to clutter the thing up and I suggest that you cut them out and paste them on a piece of cardboard.

Sophistication and smartness are, of course, the chief prerequisites. This is true not only of the drawings themselves, but of the captions for them. A drawing and its caption dovetail, or should dovetail. When they don't they are hard to figure out. We have found it advisable to have the artists do the pictures and let us think up the captions for them. An artist doesn't have to have any idea in mind when he makes a drawing for us; in fact, it is much better if he doesn't. If he starts out with a vulgar idea (and sometimes artists have vulgar ideas which they think are smart ideas) he is likely to produce a picture which no other caption in the world except his own will fit. If his caption is very vulgar even an extremely sophisticated drawing wouldn't save it. A drawing is always dragged down to the level of its caption. That's an infallible rule: a drawing is always dragged down to the level of its caption. Remember that, because we are going to come back to it in a couple of thousand words, and I'll expect you to know. A case in point is the drawing of the man and woman at the dinner table (FIGURE I). The artist's own caption for that was "Give this note to my husband and wait for an answer." Now it is conceivable that a lot of people might be amused by that, but it would not be the sort of amusement we are after. It would be a little loud, for one thing, and might be followed by some such remark on the

FIGURE I

part of the vulgar reader as "I'm a —— if that ain't the funniest ——
drawing I ever see." We don't want that. What we want is the
appreciative chuckle. Anybody can guffaw. The trouble with the
caption given above is that it is neither smart nor sophisticated, it is
just funny, screamingly funny—we grant you that. It fails because the
woman's words betray an annoyance with her husband—an annoyance which she has so far forgotten herself as to convey to a servant.
If we printed such a caption, thousands of sensitive readers would be
estranged. In cases like that we usually "tinker" the caption—that is,
try to change it about so that it will be sophisticated; or we write a
brand-new line. In this particular instance, however, the artist was so
intent on making his drawing fit his caption that he turned out a
picture which no other caption we could think of would fit. Well,
there *was* one other, but it dealt with the possibility that the husband
had suffered a stroke and that the wife was sending the note to a
physician. Such a situation would of course meet the requirements of
sophistication—nothing, in fact, could be more sophisticated than for
a woman to remain calm and decorous during dinner in the face of
a grave physical affliction—but this interpretation of the drawing gets
so far away from humor that it isn't even whimsical. No organic
ailment is funny; only accidents are funny. Yet the drawing itself is
unquestionably smart, depicting, as it does, two persons of obvious

breeding, against a background of grandeur—the grandeur of simplicity, not of gaudy display. That's exactly the kind of picture we want. The note in the woman's hand is what outlawed this particular drawing. It makes the whole thing vulgar and there are no two ways about it (counting out the physician angle).

In FIGURE II we have a similar problem. The girls themselves are smart enough, but the large begonia, which takes up so much room, caused the drawing to be thrown out and the whole idea to be abandoned, for the reason that no caption was possible which simply ignored the begonia. The artist's own caption for this drawing was:

FIGURE II

"What do you think of the new planet?"
"Begonia, ain't it?"
If you can't see why that is out, we could never tell you. We might observe, however, that two-line captions are never as smart as one-line captions. For example, the simple line "Begonia, ain't it?" would have been much smarter and might have carried the picture except that it leaves out the new planet, which the artist insisted on getting in. We agreed with him there, because the new planet is what we call a "timely subject" and we like drawings occasionally which deal, in a sophisticated way, with timely subjects.[*] We kept the picture around for weeks, tinkering with it, and meanwhile the planet not only became less and less timely but was also suspected of being merely a comet. That was a lucky break for us, in a way, because had the picture been used it would probably have come out the very day that the authenticity of the plant was questioned—that is usually our luck in such matters.

Now for a few general suggestions. *The New Yorker* prefers certain groupings of persons in its drawings, of which these are a few: two fat women; two businessmen; two middle-aged men and a young woman; a silly woman and a banker; a silly woman and a major-

*EDITOR'S NOTE: At the time of this writing's appearance, August 2, 1930, the ninth planet, Pluto, had just been discovered by Clyde Tombaugh.

general; a languid man in evening dress enormously involved with another man's wife, or not involved at all with her but suspected, nevertheless, by the husband (maybe you better let that one go); two to six eager girl friends conversing in a tea-garden; two workmen on a big clock or a scaffold; and an intoxicated wife and her sober husband at a cocktail party. To explain why all these groupings are essentially smart and sophisticated would take too long—would take all night, in fact. We pick out, as just one example, the intoxicated wife and the sober husband at a party. We had just such a picture a few months ago, in which the giddy wife says to her husband, "I told you not to let me drink." That was not my caption. My caption for that drawing was rejected, although I thought it was better than the one that was used. It was: "Haven't you proud of me that I still know who I am in the mist of all this revery?" However, all this is beside the point. I simply want to establish that there is nothing smarter than for a finely gowned, handsome woman to become cockeyed at a large formal party. A vulgarian would not be able to get away with it. In such situations vulgar people go to pieces and scream or hurt somebody. It takes that *je ne sais quoi* which we call sophistication for a woman to be magnificent in a drawing-room when her faculties have departed but she herself has not yet gone home. There is no use sending in any drawings of an intoxicated wife alone with her husband. There must be some other person in the scene, perhaps a butler, or a man under the bed, to make the thing sophisticated. Sophistication might be described as the ability to cope gracefully with a situation involving the presence of a formidable menace to one's poise and prestige (such as the butler, or the man under the bed—but never the husband).

I am sorry that I cannot explain our covers. We are not permitted to give out that information. Anyway it would involve diagrams, and a lot of references you wouldn't understand.

Wayne Van R. Vermilye
for *The New Yorker*

Speaking of Drawings . . .

Some people thought my drawings were done under water; others that they were done by moonlight. But mothers thought that I was a little child or that my drawings were done by my granddaughter. So they sent in their own children's drawings to *The New Yorker,* and I was told to write these ladies, and I would write them all the same letter: "Your son can certainly draw as well as I can. The only trouble is he hasn't been through as much." [COOKE]

*   *   *

My drawings have been described as pre-intentionalist, meaning that they were finished before the ideas for them had occurred to me. I shall not argue the point. [LIFE]

*   *   *

Speed is scarcely the noblest virtue of graphic composition, but it has its curious rewards. There is a sense of getting somewhere fast, which satisfies a native American urge. *Le dessinateur rapide* also feels he is catching fugitive moods just barely in time. This general air of urgency sometimes lends an illusion of insight, a quality usually thought of, for some reason, as coming in flashes, like lightning. Furthermore, celerity produces quantity, a factor of considerable, if deceptive, importance in a competitive world. [GARLAND]

EDITOR'S NOTE: For the source of each interview or article, please see the Notes on page 257, matching the key word at the end of each excerpt with the list's respective entry.

* * *

If all the lines of what I've drawn were straightened out, they would reach a mile and a half. I drew just for relaxation, in between writing. [BREIT]

* * *

I've been brooding about the kind of change that seems to have darkened the magazine's funny cartoons recently. There is much too much stuff about the man and woman on the raft and the two beach-combers. The first should have ended twelve years ago when the man said, "You look good enough to eat," and I thought I had ended the other one in the Ohio State *Sun-Dial* in 1917 with:
    1st Beachcomber: "What did you come here to forget?"
    2nd Beachcomber: "I've forgotten."
    . . . The best thing *The New Yorker* has ever done in comic art is the probable or recognizable caption dealing with the actual relation-ships of people in our middle-class society. All of us have had a fling at fantasy and formula, but they should never predominate. I had hoped to do a few drawings based on captions I have dug out of hell in the past two years, but I think the strain would be too much for me now. Maybe [Whitney] Darrow, who drew the picture for my "When you say you hate your species do you mean everybody?" could do this one about a long married middle-aged couple. The wife is saying, "You're always talking about how dark the future of Man is—well, what do you think I got to look forward to?" This is two years old in my head. I can't do anything now since my humor sounds like that of an assistant embalmer. [DE VRIES]

* * *

"When did you learn to draw?"
    "I don't know how to draw," Thurber says, astounded that I don't know this. "Say, if I could draw, I'd probably be starving."
    "No? Then, who does draw those men and women I see in the magazines?"
    "You're trying to make me happy," Thurber says, grimacing. "You know you don't think they're men and women. Somebody

once said that I am incapable of drawing a man, but that I draw abstract things like despair, disillusion, despondency, sorrow, lapse of memory, exile, and that these things are sometimes in a shape that might be called Man or Woman. . . ." [SHER]

* * *

People who exclaim over them as being "fine," that is, a "new or exciting form of art" or whatever else they may decide they are, almost invariably miss the fact that, essentially, most of them are funny, or supposed to be funny. Those that find them funny often do not see them as being "art." You are getting a great many of the funny ones because the fellow that selected the ones for the London show invariably picked out what he thought represented "art," "draughtsmanship"—of which I, of course, in the academic meaning of the word, have none, which lack is, in itself, one of the essential points and purposes of the way I draw—"composition," "scope," and God know what else. In doing so, he got some good ones, but not very many good ones. Anyway, not many of the most successfully funny ones.

About prices, I have never had any real notion or feeling or standard. In the first place, being essentially a writer, I find that I do not in any possible way share the emotions and mentality of artists who draw or paint. They, to me, are as alien and difficult to understand as Sally Rand [the renowned fan dancer of the period]. I have, as a matter of fact, no community of anything with artists. I originally drew, I think, to satirize and poke fun at the more pretentious artists. Once I began to share the temperament, the phoney profundities, the ah-ing and oh-ing, the extravagant praise or denunciation of this and that, the language of art criticism—exceeded in monkey business only by the criticism of music . . . I would be lost. . . . [GUMP]

* * *

. . . I think it was in 1902, however, that I did my first drawings. My father was in politics—had been all his life—and although his three sons grew up to hate politics, there was a time in our extreme youth when we were fascinated by the thought of some men being elected and others defeated. So, we used to draw pictures of men and take

JAMES THURBER

them around and ask family, friends, and strangers which one they wanted to vote for. Each of us would draw one man for President, you see, on a separate sheet of paper, and submit the three sheets to people. I was eight years old and my brother William nine. He was at that time considered the artist in the family. He used to copy, painstakingly, the Gibson pen and ink drawings. I remember nothing about the men I drew as my candidates, but William had a man named, for no reason at all, Mr. Sandusky. Mr. Sandusky was elected President almost always over the man I drew. Mr. Sandusky had a mustache, and after 34 years, I remember him well—out of hate and envy I guess. I'll show you what he looked like:

Now, I don't remember my own men well at all, but I imagine they were like this:

It is fairly easy to see why people chose to place the fate of the nation in the hands of Mr. Sandusky, rather than in the hands of my nameless candidate, a man obviously given to bewilderment, vacillation, uncertainty, and downright fear.

It is true, of course, as Ralph McCombs wrote in the *Citizen*—if it was the *Citizen* and if A Benvenuto is Ralph—that I used to draw in *Caesar's Commentaries* and also illustrated the *Manual of Arms* at Ohio State (usually with pictures of Mutt and Jeff). The divine urge rose no higher than that. I did pictures for the *Sun-Dial* when I was editor because all the artists went to war or camp and left me without any artists. I drew pictures rapidly and with few lines because I had to write most of the pieces, too, and couldn't monkey long with the drawings. The divine urge rose no higher than that. In those years, I was absolutely uninterested in the art, not only of myself, but of anybody else, from anybody else to myself. . . .

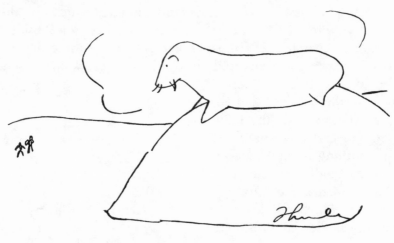

"Hm. Explorers."

It was, to be sure, E. B. White, a man given to examining everything carefully, who first began to look at my drawings critically. Like the discovery of San Salvador and the discovery of pommes soufflé the discovery of my art was an accident. I reproduce [above] the first drawing of mine ever submitted to *The New Yorker*—it was submitted by White. Naturally enough, it was rejected by an art board whose members thought they were being spoofed, if not, indeed, actually, chivvied. I got it back and promptly threw it away as I would throw away, for example, a notification from the Post Office that a package was being held there for me. That is, not exactly deliberately, but dreamily, in the course of thinking about something else. In this manner a great many of my originals have been lost. . . . [MILLER]

* * *

A few weeks ago Tom Bevans of Simon and Schuster brought me some sheets of flat black paper and a handful of white pastel chalk and, after three years, I have started plaguing *The New Yorker* with drawings once more. The men and the dogs are the same and so are the women, except that they have plunging necklines. By reversing the cuts, the drawings come out black on white. [FALL AUTHOR]

* * *

JAMES THURBER

I had a friend who was on the telephone a great deal and while he talked was always flipping the pages of his memo pad and writing things down. I started to fill up the pad with drawings so he'd have to work to get to a clean page. I began to draw a bloodhound, but he was too big for the page. He had the head and body of a bloodhound; I gave him the short legs of a basset. When I first used him in my drawings, it was as a device for balance: when I had a couch and two people on one side of a picture and a standing lamp on the other, I'd put the dog in the space under the lamp for balance.

I've always loved that dog. Although at first he was a device, I gradually worked him in as a sound creature in a crazy world. He didn't get himself into the spots that human beings get themselves into. Russell Maloney stated once that I believe animals are superior to human beings. I suspected he wanted to get me sore. If I have run down the human species, it was not altogether unintentional. They say that Man is born to the belief that he is superior to the lower animals, and that critical intelligence comes when he realizes that he is more similar than dissimilar.

Extending that theory, it has occurred to me that Man's arrogance and aggression arise from a false feeling of transcendency, and that he will not get anywhere until he realizes, in all humility, that he is just another of God's creatures, less kindly than Dog, possessed of less dignity than Swan, and incapable of becoming as magnificent an angel as Black Panther. [BREIT]

* * *

Dear Mr. Ross:

After you suggested the other day that I try to do some captions for a sheaf of [Mary] Petty drawings which seems to have stacked up almost as high as the photostatic copies of rough sketches around the office, I got to thinking that it wouldn't be a bad idea to let me spend, say, two afternoons a week in the office not only trying to write captions to pictures, but also having a look at the captions to pictures which have been bought. Since I haven't sent in an idea drawing of my own for a year and a half, my beloved art meeting could hardly say that my criticisms were based on a sheaf of my drawings having just been rejected.

You already have filed away for your autobiography some 50 or
100 blasphemous notes from me on what is the matter with the
magazine. Most of these were written, I suppose, just after I got 3 or
4 of my best drawings back. Now we are on a new basis, since I am
a blind, gray-haired playwright who still has a great affection for the
magazine and is still capable of indignation. It seems to me that
something is the matter when the first 3 drawings in the magazine
turn out the way they did in the issue of October 18 [1941]. The
parachutist, the man with the little fire extinguisher, and the man
painting the sign ("Did he want this on white or rye?") should not
have followed one right after the other. These are all definite gag
ideas and belong to the rather labored formula type. Most of the great
New Yorker captions have not had to depend on some character
holding something: a parachute, a fire extinguisher, a cat-o'-nine-tails,
or a tomahawk in the scalp. Just to quote a few of the great ones—
"I'm the one that should be lying down somewhere," "Yeh, and who
made 'em the best years?," "I want to report a winking man,"
"You're so good to me and I'm so tired of it all," "With you I have
known peace, Lida, and now you say you're going crazy"—most of
the great ones, I repeat, did not have to depend on somebody holding, wrapped up in, or pinned down by, any implement, invention,
or piece of apparatus. The really great *New Yorker* drawings have had
to do with people sitting in chairs, lying on the beach, or walking
along the street. The easy answer the art meeting always gives to the
dearth of ideas like the ones I am trying to describe is that they are
hard to get or that nobody sends them in any more. It seems to me
that the principal reason for this is that the artists take their cue from
the type of drawing which they see constantly published in the magazine. Years ago I wrote a story for *The New Yorker* in which a woman
who tried to put together a cream separator suddenly snarled at those
who were looking at her and said, "Why doesn't somebody take this
god damned thing away from me?" I want to help to take the cream
separators, parachutes, fire extinguishers, paint brushes and toma-
hawks away from four-fifths of the characters that appear in *The New
Yorker* idea drawings.

There are other things, too. It must have been 6 years ago that
you told me drawings about psychoanalysts were terribly out of date.
The next week I turned in one in which the analyst says, "A moment
ago, Mrs. Ridgway, you said that everybody you looked at seemed

to be a rabbit. Now just what did you mean by that?" You are still basically right. Drawings involving analysts have to have something fresh and different in them, such as the one I have just so modestly mentioned. But you can't publish a drawing about an analyst and a woman with the caption, "Your only trouble is, Mrs. Markham, that you're so horribly normal." This is one of the oldest, tritest, and most often repeated lines in the world. If you will look up a story of mine called "Mr. Higgins' Breakdown," published more than ten years ago, you will find that the first sentence is as follows (I quote from memory): "Gorham P. Higgins, Jr., was so normal that it took the analyst a long time to find out what was the matter with him." Just after that story appeared, the editor of *Redbook* sent for me and said he wanted me to write something for him because he had been so enchanted by that line. At that time, I have the vanity to believe, it was not old. But the years roll on, Mr. Ross, and turn into decades. So what you probably need is an old blind man sitting in one corner of Mr. Gibbs's office and snarling about certain captions which you are too old to remember helped make certain issues of *The New Yorker* way back before the depression.

Another fault of the art meeting, it seems to me, is your tendency to measure everything with rulers, stop watches, and calendars. I told Andy [E.B.] White the caption I sent in for Mary Petty and he laughed more wholeheartedly than he has since his teeth began to go and arthritis took him in the back of the neck. I understand that the art conference decided Mr. Swope was not old enough to be known to the old lady in the suggested drawing. She certainly would know old Jacob Swope's boy, Herbie, just as a woman of your mother's generation would know about Mrs. Ross's boy Harold. Furthermore, there are at least a dozen variations of that caption which I could have suggested.

If you ever write a comedy for the theatre you will discover that the best laughs invariably follow some simple and natural line which the characters involved would normally say. Thus, one of the best laughs in *The Male Animal* followed the simple statement, "Yes, you are." To show you what I mean, let's take the specific example of the drawing which appeared in the issue of October 18th in which the salesman says to the lady at the door, "Couldn't we go inside and sit down? I have a rather long sales talk." This is such an extravagant distortion of reality, it is so far removed from what any salesman would ever say, that to be successful it has to be fantastic. But since the situation is not fantastic, it ends up simply as a bad gag. All salesmen that get into drawings in *The New Yorker* ring the changes on cocksureness, ingenuity, or ignorance. When I was a little boy, in my early 20's, in Columbus, my mother opened the door one afternoon to a tall, sad salesman with a sample case, who said, "I don't suppose you want to buy any of my vanilla. Nobody ever does." There is such a thing as a tired, sad, defeated salesman, but even if there weren't we could use one. I can hear this salesman in the October 18th issue saying, "I just want to say to begin with, madam, that I have been through a great deal today." Or, "I simply must talk for a few minutes to some understanding married woman, madam. It's not about my products." I'm just batting these rough ideas out to give you an idea of how a situation and its caption can be explored, as Marc Connelly puts it. In an hour's time I could get 2 or 3 perfect captions for this particular drawing. The best laugh you get in the theatre comes from the women and as the result of hitting a universal and familiar note. The closer you come to what a human being might say, the funnier your caption is going to be. A woman laughs at a line about salesmen because it reminds her of what that funny little Fuller Brush man said to her sister Ella. No salesman ever said to any housewife what you have him saying in the cartoon I am talking about. That is a gag man's idea.

I'll talk this all over with you any time you say. I can't go on any kind of salary basis on account of the State Income Tax, but I am willing to be paid by the caption. You must feel free to reject my ideas if you don't think they are right. I just want somebody to listen to them.

Love,
THURBER [ROSS]

JAMES THURBER

Glimpses
of the Art Conference

The Art Conference discovers the work of R. Taylor.

EDITOR'S NOTE: These seven unpublished cartoons were probably executed in 1934 and refer to the once-a-week meetings of *The New Yorker*'s committee that would decide on the magazine's cartoons, spots, and illustrations.

The Art Conference decides the Dust Bowl is not known to New Yorker readers.

The funny picture is rejected because you can't tell who is talking, the old lady or the fireman, and because we had a picture of a man trying to get a drink at a dam. Besides, how did the old lady get through the police lines?

JAMES THURBER

The Art Conference buys its one hundredth drawing of 3 people on a tiny island.

Midsummer Art Conference.

COLLECTING HIMSELF

The Outside Opinion: "Is That Funny?"

Ceiling Zero.

JAMES THURBER

Matinee and Evening:

THURBER ON PLAYS AND PLAYWRITING

"The astonished hands were dancing across the family fumed heart."

Tonight at 8:30

In Mr. Coward's cycle of nine short plays, grave and gay, there are seventy characters in all, of whom Mr. Coward and Miss Lawrence together play eighteen. The settings and the time run from an autumn evening in Kent in 1860 to flats and houses in London and Mayfair of the present day, with stopovers at a country club in Samolo, the refreshment room of the Milford Junction railroad station, a villa on the Côte d'Azur, and the stage of a variety hall in a provincial English town. The plays deal, mainly, with the anatomy of love and marriage and the treatment varies from a feathery touch *(We Were Dancing)* that parodies Mr. Coward's wittiest manner to the sombre and tragic examination of a gray-haired psychiatrist drowning in the waters of a wayward passion *(The Astonished Heart)*.

Mr. Coward dresses up (and sometimes undresses) as every kind of character, from a miserable, henpecked husband of the lower classes, in *Fumed Oak,* to the courtly Victorian Jasper Featherways of *Family Album.* Miss Lawrence runs an astonishing gamut, from a slatternly frump of a wife to a beautifully gowned doll of a wife, back to a loud-tongued dancer in a cheap music hall.

Sprinkled over the plays are seven or eight songs by Mr. Coward, some graceful dancing, some vaudeville hoofing; there are costumes and sets that bring exclamations from the audience and others that start them guffawing. I remember a music box playing an old waltz, a desperate man jumping out of a window, a pair of dancers kissing, an old woman screaming, ladies in pretty dresses drinking Madeira, a husband throwing butter on the floor. It's pretty hard, at the far end of nine plays, to get at them all by a listing and an itemizing. Fortunately, in some improbable way, the whole thing hangs together as an entity: the latest work of Noel Coward in the theatre. Taking it thus boldly as a whole, I can say, without any hesitation, that I liked it; hell, I was crazy about it.

In this day of the short short story and the long long novel and the same old three-act play, Mr. Coward's medium is a refreshing change. Only two of these nine plays are done in one scene with no lowering of the curtain until the end. The others, running from two to six scenes, are short comedies and dramas; not one-act plays, not skits. At least two of them (and maybe, in Mr. Coward's facile hands, four) could have been expanded into full-length plays, but they would have been diluted and attenuated, they would have lost the sharp, quick glow he has put upon them. I got to thinking about certain three-act dramas I had seen (among them *The Petrified Forest,* no matter what you think) and wondering if they would not have profited by being cut down to an hour and a quarter (I believe Mr. Coward's own *Point Valaine* would have profited by it; a dabbing on of that strange poison might have been more persuasive than its slow application; a quicker view of Mr. Lunt with his suspenders trailing, if you remember).

Anyway, the formula Mr. Coward hit on for these particular pieces makes for three acutely pointed up evenings in the playhouse. It is a formula analagous to that which, in prose writing, Henry James called "the beautiful and blest *nouvelle,*" not so short as a short story, not so long as a novel. Mr. Coward's present form is shorter than the conventional play, longer than the one-act play. If this *nouvelle* of the theatre has its bright, particular felicities, it also has its perils: too much could be crowded out or nervously crowded in; the thing could be abrupt, jerky, and unsatisfactory. In Mr. Coward's hands it never is.

The Astonished Heart has six scenes, each lasting only ten or fifteen minutes; three of them take place in November 1935, one in November 1934, one in January 1935, and one in April 1935. The gradual emotional entanglement and spiritual disintegration of a man has to be presented in a little more than an hour. There are only a few seconds between scenes. Mr. Coward persuades you that everything you see come about has come about, lingeringly, in its time. It is a fine technical achievement. (Whether you can identify yourself thoroughly with his psychiatrist in the play is, of course, another thing.

This, Mr. Coward's favorite of his nine works, is a study of a highly specialized infatuation. It is clinical rather than familiar, and for me lacks the sure authority of the basically similar situation in *Still Life.* I have reached the time of life when I believe that men do not die for love, or the ravages of love—or maybe only that they shouldn't. There is, for my taste, a sterner and a livelier problem in the analysis of the astonished heart left tragically incapable of violence by the passions which send the muddled Dr. Christian Faber to his death. The shoulder of his wife would have been, to my mind, a more inevitable place for him to end up than the pavement below his window, and a damn sight harder place, both for the doctor and for the playwright. Which is all, perhaps, mere dialectic—or is it ideology? Anyway, let's get the hell out of this parenthesis.)

It seems to me that all these plays are written wisely and well (Mr. Coward, as you may know, bats them off in no time at all, which appalls me). His right words for those who have been long in love, or marriage, and for those who have just fallen into love, or marriage, have, at their best, a precision that moves toward the absolute. They would do, for me, as epitaphs on the loves and marriages of our time (you can go to Mr. Maugham for a harder granite or to Mr. Huxley for a colder chisel, if you want to). I remember especially the talk of the lovers in *Still Life;* it was exactly right.

Before *The Astonished Heart* comes on, Mr. Coward and Miss Lawrence have moved gaily through a very funny mix-up in a smart London drawing room, *Hands Across the Sea,* and after it is over they romp loudly through a very funny brawl in a tawdry music hall. Which brings us to the outstanding thing about our cycle of nine: the really remarkable acting of Miss Lawrence and Mr. Coward throughout. As far as I'm concerned she could play Little Eva, or even Harriet Beecher Stowe herself, and he could play Grover Cleveland. They seem to be able to do anything—indeed, in these plays, they darn near do. They're fine as the bickering Gows in *Fumed Oak* (one of my favorites); they're exact as the troubled Gayforths in *Shadow Play* (the trickiest and most fanciful of the nine); they're immensely moving as the stricken lovers in *Still Life* (the one I liked the best); they're perfect as the pictorial Featherways in *Family Album* (an enchanting half hour); they're amusingly right as the impecunious Cartwrights of *Ways and Means;* and, as the raucous Peppers of the music halls— well, you wonder they ever rose above the Palace of Varieties. Surely there are no other two who could so perfectly do all these things. I heard someone nominate Alfred Lunt and Ina Claire. They might be smart enough to do it, but I think they'd be too smart to try it.

The rest of the cast are by no means thrown into shadow; they are all very good; there is a smooth unity about everything this company does. Joyce Carey plays a variety of character parts with effective sureness; Alan Webb, in an even wider range of roles, is bound to catch your respectful attention; you will remember Edward Underdown and Moya Nugent—particularly her little Elsie in *Fumed Oak*. The credit line, "Decor by G. E. Calthrop," covers a multitude of always fitting, sometimes brilliant, sets. Miss Lawrence's gowns were exclaimed over by the ladies of Boston, where I enjoyed the Coward cycle. The audience there on the last night stood and cheered. I heard a gray-haired woman say that in twenty-eight years of Boston playgoing she had no memory of such a letting go. More decorous and self-contained than Boston folk, I did not rise and shout, but I applauded loudly and, here in this place, I do so again. I had a swell time.

(This tableau presents Mrs. Rockett [Joyce Carey], the carping mother-in-law of *Fumed Oak,* screaming at Hubert Charteris [Alan Webb], the puzzled and indignant husband of *We Were Dancing.* Elsie [Moya Nugent], the awful little child of *Fumed Oak,* here looks on dully. This scene does not happen in *Tonight at 8:30;* it just happens here.)

JAMES THURBER

Letter from the States

You are probably still trying to get tickets to *South Pacific*, and I wish you luck, but what has interested me most in the current New York theatre season is a trio of plays by three men who unquestionably belong to the literary ages. Such a display of fame and genius is not a common occurrence on Broadway. The plays are *Caesar and Cleopatra* by G. B. Shaw, a great playwright, *The Cocktail Party*, by T. S. Eliot, a great poet, and *The Turn of the Screw*, by the late Henry James, a great novelist. This last, called *The Innocents*, and written by William Archibald, is a faithful stage version of the master's famous old ghost story.

Caesar and Cleopatra is more than fifty years old, but is still as fresh as a daisy and as bright as a 1950 dollar. It has been done before, but never so brilliantly and gaily as in the present production, which stars Sir Cedric Hardwicke as Caesar, and Lilli Palmer as Cleopatra. Shaw's Caesar is not the marble-faced, laurel-wreathed fellow whose *Commentaries* turned you against him in high school, but just about the most wonderful man you ever saw on any stage or in any book. Sir Cedric makes the most of Shaw's idol, and Miss Palmer would have been executed instantly by the real Cleopatra for her beauty, her radiance, and her lovely figure. Shaw is said to have got the idea for his play after reading Mommsen's *History of Rome.* I happened to read Mommsen in Rome in 1938, but I am a Hannibal man and I skipped the chapters on Caesar.

It has always been a contention of mine that Hannibal could have beaten Caesar the best day Caesar ever saw, just as I think that Jack Johnson could have taken Gene Tunney if both men had been in their prime at the same time. I looked up the dates on Caesar and Hannibal the other day to see how far they missed each other. Hannibal had been dead eighty-three years when Caesar was born in 100 B.C. Since Caesar's expedition into Gaul was made in 58 B.C., when he was forty-two years old, something like a hundred and forty years lay between the military heydays of the two immortal generals. This is too bad. A clash between Caesar and Hannibal would have been something to translate from the Latin, always providing that Julius would have been in shape to write about it. Vercingetorix and his Gauls were just so many Primo Carneras, or antique pushovers, compared to the light and heavy cavalry of Hannibal and the storm troops that broke the center of the Roman line at Cannae. I discussed the relative merits of the two imperators with a man from V. M. I. [Virginia Military Institute] recently. He contends that Stonewall Jackson could have taken them both in the same ring, or across the same Rubicon or pass of the Little St. Bernard.

Eliot's *The Cocktail Party* quickly became the talk of the town after it opened early this year. Even its producers hadn't held out much hope for the American success of a play in verse written by a distinguished poet famous, even among the literati, for the profundity of his thought and the difficulty of his meanings. The play became an instant hit, somewhat to the surprise of everybody. Anti-intellectuals, haters of poetry, and other Philistines who go to the play expecting to endure an ordeal find themselves under the spell of a new and strange enchantment. A voice of unique authority speaks from the astonished Broadway stage, in subtle and magical rhythms that make even the businessman, dragged to the play by his wife, lean forward and listen. Eliot himself has said that his play means anything its audiences think it means, and this has led American theatregoers, who love argument and debate, to plunge loudly and freely into the general controversy *The Cocktail Party* has aroused. There are even those who claim to know more about the true meaning of the play than Eliot does. He would be the last to disagree with them. It is played by a perfect cast of English actors who have the fine flexibility of instruments in an orchestra.

No story in the past hundred years has aroused more controversy among literary critics and literary psychiatrists than Henry James's *The Turn of the Screw,* which Mr. Archibald has transcribed for the theatre with devotion and sensitive understanding. There are six in the cast, including the ghosts of Peter Quint and Miss Jessel, who are properly left unlisted in the program, out of broadminded deference to those grim and relentless critics and psychiatrists who do not believe there are any ghosts in the story. The literature of controversy as to the meaning and motivation of *The Turn of the Screw* is voluminous. Is it a simple, but subtle, story, deliberately created by a great artist, about the ghosts of two servants who came back from hell to capture and corrupt the souls of a twelve-year-old boy and an eight-year-old girl in a dark English manor house of the late nineteenth century, or is it the unconscious projection, in Freudian symbolism, of the tortured psyche and the inner conflict of a complicated human being named Henry James? The Freudian literary critics and the Freudian literary psychiatrists, who are becoming more and more literary by the hour, find that the story falls into a fairly familiar pattern of human experience, when the searchlights of psychiatry are turned on it, but those of us who believe in the independent selective power of the artistic intelligence cannot be overwhelmed by their arguments, even though we accept the basic assumptions of the followers of Freud. It is interesting to note that Freud himself held that the creative artist was beyond this full and facile taking apart, but his successors think nothing of dividing the magnificent intelligence of Henry James into a few simple causes and effects.

However all this may be, Mr. Archibald has stuck loyally to

James's belief that his ghosts are real ghosts. He has written a play of charm, fascination, and quiet excitement, and if it doesn't always have the dark depths and special eloquence of the original story, it is nevertheless a play that holds you in the theatre and haunts you afterwards. It is superbly acted by an English boy of thirteen and a nine-year-old American girl, who seem to have something greater than an adult understanding of the secrets and shadows that walk in the garden, peer through the windows, and inhabit the halls of the house with thirty-five rooms, most of them locked. The two grown women who support the precocious youngsters are brave indeed to take on such a thankless task.

JAMES THURBER

A Farewell to Santa Claus

(OR, VIOLINS ARE NICE
FOR BOYS WITH CHINS)

(The idea of this playlet grew gradually in the mind of the writer while he was quietly trying to read Chekhov's *Notebooks* at a cocktail party where the guests were discussing Hemingway, while one man in a lady's hat was imitating Ed Wynn.)

[*It is Christmas Eve. Santa Claus, in a patched suit, is working on a wooden toy, using only a gouge, for he has had to sell his other tools. In one corner his wife is dying of grief; in another corner a student is attempting suicide. Enter from time to time several Italian army officers and Russian government clerks.*]

SANTA CLAUS: This toy is no good.

JUNIOR CLAUS: I am cold.

MRS. CLAUS: Hush.

STUDENT: What, no prosperity! [*Shoots self.*]

ARMY OFFICER: It's no good flying all over the world with one toy.

SANTA CLAUS: As each child reaches for it, I will pull it back up the chimney. It will teach them they can't even trust Santa Claus.

JUNIOR: I am hungry.

MRS. CLAUS [*rocking back and forth, keening*]: When I was a young woman, I married a prominent myth. I ceased to believe in him and he no longer existed. Then my son believed, and my husband existed again.

JUNIOR: I don't believe in him. [*Santa Claus vanishes.*]

CLERK: I believe in him. [*Santa Claus reappears.*]

SANTA CLAUS: Cut it out. This toy is no good.

MRS. CLAUS: Never make toys, Junior. Make practical things. Your father will teach you to make practical things.

SANTA CLAUS: I don't know how to make practical things. I know how to make toys.

JUNIOR [*whining*]: I don't want to make toys. I want to make practical things.

SANTA CLAUS: All right, I'll teach you to make practical things, but they're not going to *look* like practical things.

OFFICER: It's going to be a hard winter. It's no good having a hard winter. The reindeer will die of cold.

SANTA CLAUS: The reindeer are no good.

JUNIOR: I want to kill a storekeeper. I want to shoot myself.

CLERK [*going to window*]: It is raining.

OFFICER [*moodily, holding up piece of rope*]: I have either lost a horse or am about to hang myself.

MRS. CLAUS: I don't like the rain. I am afraid of the rain.

CLERK: It is no good having rain.

SANTA CLAUS: It is time to go. [*Santa puts on an old hat and an old coat, and puts his one toy in an old bag. He whistles for his reindeer.*]

MRS. CLAUS: I am afraid of the rain.

FIRST REINDEER [*putting nose in doorway*]: I am no good.

MRS. CLAUS: Nothing is any good.

SANTA CLAUS: Which deer are you? You all look so much alike.

REINDEER: I am Vixen. Who are *you*?

SANTA CLAUS [*aside*]: He doesn't know me. I have grown so thin and emaciated; I am so gaunt and pale. [*to the reindeer*] You know me. I'm sure you know me. Look. [*He smiles in a pathetic attempt at jollity, tries to shake his sides like a bowl of jelly, blows out his sunken cheeks.*] See? Remember?

[*The reindeer studies him in a puzzled way for a few moments, then brightens slightly, and points a hoof at him.*]

REINDEER: Are you a short, fat man?

JAMES THURBER

[*Outside, sleighbells are ringing and bits of torn-up pencil-tablets, shaded to represent rain, drift by the window.*]

SANTA CLAUS: Well, I'm off. Nothing ever happens to the brave.

[*He swings his bag, with the one toy in it, over his shoulder, whistles with affected cheer, goes over to kiss Mrs. Claus, and finds she has died of grief. He stands looking at her. He doesn't say anything.*]

SANTA CLAUS [*slowly*]: Her word was law. It's like saying goodbye to a statute.

[*He walks to a hotel in the rain.*]

JUNIOR: I'm hungry.

ITALIAN OFFICER: Eat some cheese.

JUNIOR: I don't like cheese. Cheese is for rats.

OFFICER [*angrily*]: Let the rats have it.

[*Machine-gun fire offstage. All fall riddled except one government clerk. He hangs himself from the chimney with a stocking. Not a creature is stirring.*]

[CURTAIN]

*"I had the strangest feeling in the elevator
that I was changing into Clare Luce."*

"Well, I've found Miss Gish for you, Mr. Freeman.
No relation to the sisters, incidentally."

*"Slip something on, Mrs. Parks, and take a look at the new
Warner Brothers sign."*

JAMES THURBER

One Man in His Time

Everything from chagrin to humiliation has happened to me in the long years of my going to see Eugene O'Neill's plays. For instance, I remember how the lovely young lady who accompanied me to *The Emperor Jones,* out in Columbus, persisted in believing that the curtain-raiser, that old chestnut *Suppressed Desires,* was the first act of the tragedy. We drifted gradually apart after that until we came to the point where we simply exchanged Christmas cards. Then there was the humiliating moment during a performance of *The Hairy Ape* when my uncle Jake Schoaf, who hadn't seen a show since the Hanlons' *Superba* in 1907 and who was no longer able to lend himself to the illusion of make-believe, crawled halfway over the footlights before the bull-fiddle player and two ushers could pull him down. Jake had taken as a personal reflection on his own courage and strength some of the wild speeches of Yank in the play.

All this is simply by way of introduction to my rather confused feelings about the new O'Neill play, *Days Without End,* which I haven't yet got up the courage to go and see but which I have been reading about. Instead of making one man become two men, simply by putting on and taking off a mask, or standing still and talking in a flat monotone and then moving around and talking in a natural voice, he has made two men become one man. There is, as the old saying goes, no use in crying over split personalities, but nevertheless the breaking up of a man into himself and his alter ego moves me. I may not exactly cry about it, but I worry about it, and I find that in this case it has moved me to endless speculations.

One of my speculations has been about a certain similarity between Mr. O'Neill's devices in the drama and Henry James's strategies in his later novels. They have at least one thing in common—an "indirectness of narrative technique," as Ludwig Lewisohn has called it. Had Mr. James lived another ten years, he might conceivably have got so far away from direct narration that instead of simply telling what occurred when two persons came together, he would have presented it through the consciousness of a Worcester, Massachusetts, lawyer who got it from the proprietor of a café who had overheard two people at a table piecing together a story they had listened in on at a large and crowded party. The difference between the indirectness of James and that of O'Neill lies in the fact that whereas James got farther and farther away from his central character by filtering that central character through the perceptions of other people, O'Neill achieves his remoteness of contact by having his central character get farther and farther away from himself through splitting up into various phases of viewpoint and behavior.

Of course, O'Neill has not as yet carried out this device to its ultimate expression, and I am very much afraid, therefore, that it is the object of this essay, once it gets going, to suggest and outline that ultimate expression. Let us take, then, a hypothetical play to be called "One Man in His Time," which is concerned with the splitting up into twelve or fifteen separate personalities of a famous retired surgeon named Gregori.

This Gregori is a moody, violent man, given to long hours of profound melancholy which explodes at intervals into veritable orgies of ecstatic self-oblivion, on which occasions there appear at his otherwise lonely estate (The Cypresses) seven or eight men friends, all of whom turn out to be himself. I have selected Wallace Beery to play the part of the original and basic ego, Dr. Gregori, whom we meet in the first scene obviously losing his grip on reality. In walks a young lad who is Gregori at seventeen, or rather Gregori's memory of himself at seventeen. The young lad does not discern in this crumbling man the fine flower of middle age which he aspires to become. On the contrary, he mistakes for his mature self a tutor (played by Leslie Howard) who is tutoring Gregori's lovely but diverse young ward (played by Miriam Hopkins, Fannie Brice, Margalo Gillmore, Margaret Wycherly, and Katharine Cornell). The tutor (Mr. Howard) is, in reality—that is, such reality as we have—

the Gregori that the young lad dreams of becoming, the alter ego which still resides deep within the main Gregori (Wallace Beery). The tutor is handsome but frail, and obviously is not going to be alive at the end of the play's two tremendously long acts.

Now the alter ego (Mr. Howard), observing with jealousy that the lovely ward, when she is Miriam Hopkins, is more drawn to the rowdy and dissolute Gregori (Mr. Beery) than she is to him, alternately tries to laugh off his love for her (at which times she becomes Fannie Brice) and to keep her on a kind of platonic and academic pedestal (Margalo Gillmore). The tutor's desire for the young ward's lovely body (Miss Hopkins) evokes in him a feeling of guilt (played by Ernest Milton right up to the hilt). This guilt (Mr. Milton) keeps following Mr. Howard around, doing exactly what he does, imitating every gesture, repeating every word, mockingly—*but only, however, when Miss Hopkins is also on stage.* When Miss Brice is on stage and Mr. Howard enters, he is followed, or "shadowed," by a Gregorian phase of boisterous devil-may-care (Mr. Bobby Clark), and when Miss Gillmore has scenes with Mr. Howard, there follows him, wherever he moves, Gregori's sporadic and tortured determination to resign himself to a life of academic tutoring entirely divorced from emotional content (Mr. Laurence Olivier).

The first act reaches its high point when, after a terrific wrestling bout with Bobby Clark and sharp, high words with Mr. Milton, Mr. Howard throws them both off and takes Miss Hopkins passionately into his arms (terribly hampered by Mr. Milton, who is trying grotesquely to do the same thing). The basic Gregori (Mr. Beery) enters and for the first time sees clearly what the latent best side of himself (Mr. Howard) has become, a man who is about to gave up all intellectual ambitions and obligations for the pleasures of the flesh. He (Beery) tries to ignore the struggle going on between Mr. Howard, Miss Hopkins, and Mr. Milton by getting drunk in a lusty knockabout scene with Miss Brice, at the end of which he flings her, face down, upon a sofa. Beery exits, taking the sense of guilt (Mr. Milton) with him, leaving Mr. Howard and Miss Hopkins in a now completely abandoned attitude of surrender to each other. They are about to fling themselves together upon the sofa when they discover the woman's form lying there. Miss Hopkins, disentangling herself, pulls the woman off the sofa and the audience sees that she is no longer Fannie Brice but Margalo Gillmore! (This is going to be easier to do in the movies than on the stage.) Miss Hopkins flies at her, but Miss Gillmore, erect and cool and wholesome, bids her, with imperious sweetness, please to go, which reluctantly she does, clenching and unclenching her hands. As the curtain starts down, Miss Gillmore begins to repeat her history lesson to Mr. Howard, in a low, steady voice, while Mr. Olivier, standing behind Mr. Howard, sobs quietly.

In the second act, Mr. Beery, who has been drinking all night, is discovered, singing and swearing and guzzling, with those seven or eight "friends" who are, as we know but he doesn't, the seven or eight ugly phases of himself that "come out" when he is in one of his orgies. During this particular orgy, which lasts all of the act, Mr. Howard falls desperately ill. Miss Hopkins, for whom he is calling piteously off stage, ignores him and joins Beery and his guests at their carousing. The ward's maternal instinct (Miss Wycherly) appeals to Miss Hopkins to go to Howard or at least to quit drinking with Beery, but to no avail. Mr. Milton now comes on, pale and stricken, and begs Beery to come with him. "Dr. Gregori," says Milton, "if you do not perform an immediate operation, he cannot live!" Beery, in his cups, at first refuses, but at the last, urged by Miss Gillmore, Miss Brice, and Miss Wycherly, all chanting in unison: "You must go, you must go, you must go!," rises from his chair, girds up his loins, and says he will go. At this moment, his natural indecisiveness (Mr. Henry Hull) steps up, in the costume of a butler, and proffers him a bottle of fine brandy which has just been delivered to his door as a gift. Mr. Beery uncorks it, and tries to pour some of it into a glass. He misses the glass, and spills the brandy on the floor. He gazes at his quivering hands, aghast. He is no longer able to save his better self (Leslie Howard). Cursing the butler, he flings the bottle at him, but hits Mr. Olivier instead. Miss Gillmore rushes to his side. "I'm afraid it's too late to save him," she says quietly. "Who?" demands Beery, reaching for another glass. "Does it matter?" asks Miss Gillmore. There is a little groan off stage—from Gregori's better self (Mr. Howard)—and all rush off except Beery and his seven or eight drunken phases. He turns on them. "You brought me to this!" he roars. "You brought me to this!" they echo, in unison. "I swear to God you did!" he roars. "I swear to God you did!" they echo. In the midst of this, which rises higher and higher, the young ward staggers slowly back onto the

JAMES THURBER

stage, a tragic, blasted woman (Katharine Cornell). "Everybody seems," she says in a slow, hollow voice, which quiets the shouting of Beery and his phases, "to be dead." The curtain comes down.

That is as far as I have been able to get with the thing. There is much in my first rough draft that I have had to leave out, including the entrance, at one point, of Mr. Lionel Barrymore and Mr. Ernest Truex, who are joined together at the waist with a linked iron chain. It sounds significant and impressive, but I have forgot just what conflict in Gregori they were supposed to represent. Perhaps it is just as well.

Is There a Killer
in the House?

I am not what authorities would call an authority on mystery melo-dramas made from popular detective fiction—my specialities happen to be bloodhounds, holy matrimony, monsters, and modern English misusage—but I have sat through more than a score of such plays in the past thirty-five years, from Mary Roberts Rinehart's *The Bat,* which I saw in Columbus, Ohio, when I was still in my twenties, to Agatha Christie's *The Mousetrap,* which I listened to here in London at a recent Saturday matinee, when I was sixty.

I began going to plays in Columbus in 1905, at the age of 11, paying ten cents for an unreserved seat in what we called "The Peanut Roost" or "Nigger Heaven," and I must have seen a hundred dramas and comedies, or about ten-dollars worth, before I was out of my teens. I wasn't interested in mystery plays then, preferring Western shows, such as *The Round Up, The Great Divide, The Squaw Man,* and *Arizona,* and Civil War plays like *Dixie, Secret Service, Shen-andoah,* and *Barbara Frietchie.* My father occasionally dragged me to see Mantell, Mansfield, and Sothern, but none of them seemed to me so gifted as Maclyn Arbuckle who, at the end of the second act of *The Round Up,* rolled a Bull Durham cigarette with one hand, thus establishing himself, in my estimation, as the greatest actor of his time. It wasn't until 1920 that the mystery plays began flowering, or running up like weeds, and in addition to *The Bat* I saw a dozen others, including *The Thirteenth Chair, The Silent Witness,* and *The Cat and the Canary.* (This last was made into a movie in 1939, in which

Bob Hope played the hero with an air of such sinister wistfulness that I was convinced he was the murderer, and still stick doggedly to that theory.)

The maturing mind may be measured, in part, by its changing attitude toward mystery plays. One should begin with a desire to be puzzled, go on to a determination to out-think the playwright, and end up with a healthily morbid hope that something will go wrong during a performance. I was pleasurably fooled by *The Bat,* easily figured out that the telephone in *The Silent Witness* was going to be the murder weapon, and enjoyed most of all the lovely mishaps that occurred on the first night of a thing called *Shooting Shadows.* This one shot itself to death (in New York, in 1926) at the end of the second act, to my vast delight. Two pistols were supposed to go off simultaneously, making a single loud report, one of them on stage and the other off, but the one on stage missed fire and the one in the wings sounded like the last cannon at Gettysburg. The third act was anti-climax of a high order, but it had another wonderful moment, when a woman character, understandably nervous, screamed, "The hand! The hand!," staring at an eerie clutching human hand that was supposed to be protruding horribly through a drapery. The trouble was that the owner of the hand was still in his dressing room or somewhere, and the drama took on at this point a beautifully unplanned tone of hallucination. Everything unfortunately went all right during the rest of the run, which lasted five nights and one matinee.

There may be something wrong with a 60-year-old man who attends mystery plays, praying that God will reward him with some manifestation of the untoward, and I began scolding myself at *The Mousetrap* for this perversely devout attitude and trying to trace its origin. (After all, I had identified the killer at about twenty-five-minutes to six, and had nothing else to do.) I think I traced it, all right. In 1923, I had written the libretto for a College musical comedy called *The Cat and the Riddle,* a burlesque of the mystery plays of the period, which died of a strange surfeit of light at its opening performance in Columbus. The stage lights were supposed to black out for ten seconds near the end of Act I, in order to cover up the transfer of a gun and conceal the identity of the killer, but the lights stayed on. The cast of inexperienced University players went right ahead with the business, anyway, and with another act and a full hour still to go, the sheriff was revealed to the audience as the cat in a veritable glare of revelation, and there wasn't a Riddle any more.

The distinguished American-Irish author John McNulty, then drama critic for a Columbus paper, sent me a touching note of condolence the following day, which I still remember. "I was hilariously grieved," he wrote, "to hear that your musical comedy was taken suddenly dead last night at the age of one act. I happened to be weeping for Adonais when I heard the news, but now I am weeping for you."

Now that I have so courageously confessed, in public, what is the matter with me at mystery plays, I can return to *The Mousetrap* in an easier frame of mind.

Mr. Edmund Wilson, the American literary critic, alienated thousands of detective fiction addicts a few years ago when he manhandled almost all the celebrated mystery novels, in the Book Department of *The New Yorker* magazine. He found merit only in the works of Raymond Chandler, and discovered nothing to interest him in such notable classics as *The Maltese Falcon, The Murder of Roger Ackroyd, The Circular Staircase, Trent's Last Case, The Yellow Room,* and *The Murder of My Aunt,* to name half-a-dozen which connoisseurs usually consider the finest and most original of the thousands that have been written. Mr. Wilson concluded that the reading of detective stories was a minor vice, comparable to the smoking of cigarettes. (This was before the smoking of cigarettes became a major vice.) I doubt that Mr. Wilson could now remember the plots of any of the books he read at the time, and thus he would probably be unable to determine which of the classic novels *The Mousetrap* paraphrases—if that is the word for it. This piece becomes a trifle aimless since the rules of the game—and very strict rules they are, too—prevent me from telling. The traditional taboo limits criticism almost to the point of elimination, and it had some singular effects on theatregoing in my home city years ago. I had seen Shaw's *Saint Joan* in New York and when it came to Columbus, a cousin of mine there asked me if I thought he would enjoy it, hastily adding: "Don't tell me how it comes out." Incidentally, Porter Emerson Browne's non-mystery comedy *The Bad Man* disappointed many Columbus playgoers because the man who was obviously the killer turned out actually to be the killer. This confusion was surpassed only during the road tour of *The Emperor*

Jones, when many mystery play fans mistook the old curtain-raiser *Supressed Desires* for the first act of the O'Neill play.

I know, to my amazement, a number of persons who have read at least 3,000 mystery novels in the past fifteen years and still remain unconfined in institutions for the mentally upset. They know all the hundreds of different twists of plot and of "gimmick," including what Hollywood calls the switcheroo and the switcherino, and what I call the switcherissimo. They are experts not only on who did it, but on how it could be done when it couldn't. The immemorial gadgetry of the mystery medium includes the wolf in police dog's clothing, the discarnate voice, the would-be killer who changes places with the going-to-be victim, the guilty narrator or homicidal Dr. Watson, the weapon that vanishes, the body that gets up and walks, the two men who are one man, and the one man who is two. Some new variants, such as that of the locked room, are admissible, because ingenuity makes up paraphrase and permutation, but it has always seemed to me that the identity of a few classic types of killer will not stand up under repetition. Even as I write, however, some gifted author may be at work on a mystery play in which you will know it is not the butler all the time, and it turns out to be the butler.

Agatha Christie does not often fail, and I think that *The Mousetrap* is the only opus of hers that I ever figured out. Her success is proved not only by the fact that one million copies in all, of ten of her books, were reprinted in 1948, and another million of ten others about five years later, but by the equally astounding fact that *The Mousetrap* is now in its third year at the Ambassador Theatre. How ingenuity and flexibility of contrivance can stand up under such a flow of fecundity is a marvel to a writer who is hard put to it to invent two or three small plots in a year and a half. Mrs. Christie is, of course, the author of one of the six classics I have listed above, *The Murder of Roger Ackroyd,* whose central device does not lend itself to reworking by other hands, but other hands have no doubt reworked it. The list of her other inventions would fill a column, and get us nowhere.

Mrs. Christie is a mystery writer and dramatist content, as a rule, to place narrative above or, if you will, below literature, and she can write so fast as to become charmingly ungrammatical, as in this sentence from *The Regatta Murders*—I think that's it—"the guilt lies between one of us in this room." As a man between whom guilt often lies heavily, I have remembered that line for fifteen-years. But then, on the other hand, she can write a fine comic speech, in good English, such as that of Counsel for the Defence in her *Witness for the Prosecution* which goes like this: "If my learned adversary is going to answer his own questions, I suggest that the presence of the witness is superfluous." I do not propose, let me say at once, to start an argument with myself about the comparative literary merits of the authors of mysteries. It is common knowledge, however, that Dashiell Hammett and Raymond Chandler are writers of high ability, each with his unique talent and special forcefulness. No less severe critic than Mr. Elmer Davis selected Chandler's *The Long Goodbye* as one of the three books of any kind that interested him most last year. And if you haven't read Hammett, from *The Dain Curse* through *The Glass Key,* you have missed quite a lot.

I note, with some regret, that one of my favorites, Margery Allingham, has abandoned the kind of thing she delighted me with so much in *The Case of the Late Pig,* for more serious stuff. Bringing literature to mystery stories is a hard trick indeed, and it is perhaps better to bring mystery to literature, as in the case of several of the books of the late Josephine Tey. She does not stick to the stern rules of mystery devices, and sometimes doesn't even have anybody killed, as in *The Franchise Affair,* which seems to me a novel of some sociological importance, as well as a wonderfully easy book to read. In *The Daughter of Time* her Inspector Grant lies on a hospital bed throughout the narrative and really has nothing to do with it. He simply supervises at a vast immobilized distance a process of careful and intricate deduction at the end of which Richard III emerges as a kindly gentleman who never murdered anybody. (This book was partly, but not entirely, responsible for the formation of the American Society, of which I am a member, called "Friends of Richard III.")

I see I've left out of my list of gimmicks, the fake impostor, or self-impersonator. This character turned up a few seasons ago in a New York mystery play called *The Visitor* and most of us first-night bloodhounds had him spotted by five-minutes after nine o'clock. At this point the late Robert Benchley dozed off in his seat, to be awakened by a ringing phone upon which the second act curtain rose. It rang for twenty-seconds on an empty stage, or about five-minutes as theatre time goes, and a restive audience was exhilarated when Mr. Benchley woke and was heard to say: "Why doesn't someone answer that? I think it's for me." This got into the reviews next day as perhaps the brightest moment of the evening, but the producer of *The Visitor* was not pleased. He turned in dismay to his press agent, the fabulous Richard Maney, and said that Bob Benchley's performance had not helped the play. To this, Mr. Maney replied, promptly and astutely: "Benchley is not what's the matter with *The Visitor.*"

When this critique—if that's what it is—appears, I shall be in Scotland under an assumed name, and it will be no use trying to find me. It would take an English bloodhound to do that, and the English Police, I have discovered to my surprise and sorrow, do not employ bloodhounds.

Producers
Never Think Twice

Readers of the Broadway gossip columns in the newspapers must have come across the recent announcement that Joan Crawford and Franchot Tone would like to act the leading rôles in a dramatization of James M. Cain's *The Postman Always Rings Twice,* that stark, passionate, and earthy story of lust and murder at a hot-dog stand in California. The announcement of the strange desire of these wistful, romantic screen lovers was brief and not very explicit. It was hard to make out—from the paragraphs *I* read, anyway—whether Joan and Franchot want to do *The Postman* on the stage or in the movies or both. Both, I daresay. It is, however, the visualization of the charming twain in a movie version of the tough, knockabout novel which has engrossed my imagination since I read the disturbing little item. I have even gone so far as to outline the action and dialogue of the first reel of the movie, which I have given the working title of "Love Lasts Forever."

The first scene is the interior of an elegant and handsomely appointed hot-dog stand and filling station on a highway in California. (The set will be so arranged that when the action gets too dull, W. C. Fields can enter from the left, or from anywhere else, with an armful of cigar boxes, a golf club, or a kadoola-kadoola.) Tables are tastefully arranged here and there, covered with fine napery and lighted by pale-yellow candles in gleaming silver candlesticks. The whole place looks rather more like the drawing-room of a Long Island country estate than a hot-dog stand. This is because the Greek who runs the joint has made a great deal of money out of hot dogs and gasoline, and Miss Crawford, as his wife, has persuaded him, by God only knows what bitter surrenders of her delicate person, to allow her to fix the place up a little.

Miss Crawford (and I shall hereinafter call her Joan, and Mr. Tone Franchot, because I have forgotten the names of the characters in the book) is discovered daintily clearing up a table at which some garage hand has just been eating a couple of hamburgers. Joan would keep such riffraff out of the place if she could, but her husband, the Greek, is just a dumb, materialistic hot-dog-stand proprietor and will not listen to her. She is clad in a green tweed suit with a fetching irregular jacket hem and a collar of breit-schwanz, the whole topped by a modernized Directoire bonnet.

Enter the Greek in a shiny blue-serge suit, yellow shoes, and a silk shirt with an old-fashioned detachable celluloid collar into which he has loosely knotted a yellow, flowered tie. He is a crude fellow, with a kind of senseless amiability and none of the finer sensibilities at all.

GREEK: Whatsa matta?

JOAN: Won't you *please* refrain from addressing me always as Whatsa Matta? One would think, if one thought about it, that I were a servant of some sort, a menial—but one never thinks about it. No one *ever* thinks of me save you, and then in terms of either gross attention or neglect.

GREEK: Kissa you, huh? [*He comes toward her and she shrinks away.*]

JOAN: Does your mind never dwell on anything higher?

GREEK: [*still amiable, but a little puzzled*]: I go buy a new neon sign. Dat's higha. Good-a-bye. [*He exits, singing.*]

Joan goes into a pantomime of staring out a window and indicating that she is lonely, misunderstood, frustrated, unhappily married to a Greek hot-dog-stand proprietor, love-starved, and on the verge of a kind of pensive desperation. She exits to her boudoir, and W. C. Fields comes on with an armful of cigar boxes. He is dressed in an unpressed, rusty-black ensemble, with old plug hat to match, and he does his cigar-box-juggling acts and exits. Joan comes back on wearing a black moiré bagheera gown with Medici ruff and train, her neck and wrists encircled by Mauboussin jewels. She stands at the door looking wistfully up the road. It is growing dark, but she apparently discerns an approaching figure, and hastily retires to her boudoir again.

Enter Franchot, the wanderer, who has just been playfully thrown from a Rolls-Royce by a party of madcap millionaire playboys and their débutante friends. He is dressed in a handsome and well-fitting riding habit, silver spurs, jodhpurs, elegant silver-tipped riding crop, etc. He sits down at a table. Joan comes back into the room dressed in a black faille taffeta evening gown, the skirt sophisticatedly sheathed to the knees, from where it flares out charmingly toward the hemline; she wears gold-and-black evening sandals.

JOAN: I had not seen you until now.

FRANCHOT: Nor I you. Yet I somehow felt your presence here. It was as if I had come into a room where but lately had lingered the fragrance of some curious and disturbing exotic flower.

JOAN: [*pensively*]: Yes. That was I. Won't you sit down? If you wish to dine, I—I am desolated to tell you that we have only *les francfortois, le jambon,* and, *les steaks Hambourg; avec,* of course, *café*—either *nature* or *à la crème.*

FRANCHOT: You are too wonderful for this place. Really, you know, I am not hungry—that is, for anything so material as food. I could feast upon your beauty.

JOAN: You must not say such things, although I, too, God knows, feel this strange desire—this desire to have my beauty feasted upon by you. [*Franchot makes a slight, graceful movement toward her, but she eludes him.*]

JOAN: [*laughing, but rather sadly*]: I will get you a hot—a *chien chaud.* It will be better that way. [She exits to kitchen.]

FRANCHOT: [*reverently, moving slowly after her*]: She makes me feel as though I were in an extremely soigné gambling casino at midnight, possibly the casino at Monte Carlo. [*He exits to the washroom.*]

Joan returns in an enchanting bon-bon-pink chiffon dress with a silver yoke on the cape. She rushes to the door as if she feared the wanderer had departed, but hearing a step behind her she turns and confronts Franchot, who has reentered, dressed in a dashing polo outfit, stick and all. They approach each other slowly, their eyes deeply entangled, and suddenly without a word they go into a slow waltz. They stop, breathless, and stare at each other.

JAMES THURBER

FRANCHOT: For me all the stars in the sky have flowered and until the day I die I shall be yours and you mine.

JOAN: I love you as a child loves its first snowfall, a soft white dreamy love that will never vanish. Let us waltz again, for I am insatiate. [*They waltz again.*]

FRANCHOT: We must leave this horrible place immediately, never to return, forever to be together.

JOAN: I would go to the ends of the earth with you, but—you see, there is my husband.

FRANCHOT: What infamous cur would dare espouse one so young, so innocent, so well educated, and so ineffable as you!

JOAN: I was espoused when but a child by a Greek hot-dog-stand proprietor. At first it was glamorous, strange, wonderful—and then—then I *knew.* [*Franchot turns away for a moment.*] He is a beast whose attentions to me consist almost altogether of slapping me heavily on the back as if I were a fellow hot-dog-stand proprietor—which as God is my witness I am in name only—and saying, "Whatsa matta?" *Whatsa* matta, *whatsa* matta, *whatsa* matta!—day and night until I think sometimes I shall go mad! *Whatsa* matta? *Every*thing's the matta, *every*thing! [*She ends up sobbing, and Franchot takes her in his arms, delicately.*]

FRANCHOT: I wish Fate had so arranged it that you and I had met before you met him. Then we could have had each other.

JOAN [*fiercely*]: There is one way still!

FRANCHOT: You mean—?

JOAN: [*hoarsely*]: Come with me and I will explain. [*She leads him to the boudoir and, as the strains of waltz music come faintly from offstage, W. C. Fields enters, wearing the same ensemble he was wearing before and carrying a golf club. He goes through his golfing act.*]

That is as far as I have got with the scenario. You can go on with it if you want to.

Roaming
in the Gloaming

Science has not yet discovered why a man who has a good stomach, a great many things to do, and enough to live on should suddenly decide to write a play. Science has zipped the atom open in a dozen places, it can read the scrawlings on the Rosetta stone as glibly as a literary critic explains Hart Crane, but it doesn't know anything about playwrights. It is only fair to say that neither do I.

"Well, why did you write a play, Mr. T.?" (There will be voices coming into this at intervals.)

All I can say is that the idea came to me one day in October 1938, while I was standing on top of a garage. Whether the idea was there and I walked into it or whether I unconsciously took the idea there, I do not know; no one knows. Sometimes I think I had the basic idea eight years ago; sometimes I say it was ten. And then, at other times, I think it came to me on top of this garage. The play, as it happens, has nothing to do with garages. This is one of the soundest things about it. It doesn't even have anything to do with typewriters, although at one time that's all there was in it. You see, there was this pretty wife who could fix her husband's typewriter when it began to act that funny way. You sort of began with that: the husband all tied up in a typewriter ribbon, like the Corticelli kitten.

EDITOR'S NOTE: During the long run of *The Male Animal,* Thurber wrote several times about his experiences in the theatre with his collaborator Elliott Nugent.

JAMES THURBER

"You'll have to cut that out—nobody knows what the Corticelli kitten is."

"Well, let's just say 'tied up in a typewriter ribbon.' "

"That isn't funny."

"Cuts out four words and we're long now."

"Let's cut out the whole typewriter scene. We aren't going anywhere with it."

It is very hard for a man who has never had anywhere to go to begin going somewhere. That is, it is very hard for a man who has always just sort of started to write pieces and begun to make scrawls on paper, wondering what they were going to turn into, to encounter what is known as the three-act play. The three-act play has sharp, concrete edges, rigid spacings, a complete dependence on time, and more than eleven hundred rules, all basic. "You can't run a first act fifty minutes"; "you can't have people just sitting and talking"; "you can't play comedy in a dim light"; "you can't keep people in the theatre after 11:07 o'clock"; "anybody can write a first act"; "if you have trouble with your third act there is something the matter with your first act"; "vision is lost in revision"; "where there is no revision the playwrights perish."

These rules you learn from doormen, ushers, actors' cousins, stagehands, property men, and the little old woman in the shawl who wanders into rehearsal under the impression that she is in Schrafft's or Lord & Taylor's.

The little old woman in the shawl bends over you, heavy with suggestions, as you sit in the dark auditorium listening to actors repeat lines which, after you have heard them 186 times, seem to have no bearing whatsoever on the English language. They all sound like this: "If you had not semestered the spoons, we could have silvered this up." "If I had not semestered the spoons! The decided ash is all I have to revolve, personally!" The little old lady at this point whispers: "He should say, 'Snows are the wear of Lester's Lear.' "

For a writer in his middle years, who has learned to write slowly and not too often, who sometimes puts a piece by for a year or two because he doesn't have the slightest idea what to say on page 3, and has no desire to say it even if he could think of it, it is not the easiest thing in the world to have someone whirl around and say, "Give me a new line for Joe right here." "Hm?" says the middle-aged writer. "You don't mean today, do you?" "I mean right now!"

In this familiar theatrical crisis a curious psychological thing happens to me. The only lines I can think of are lines from other plays: "Please God, make me a good actor, goodbye Mr. Chips! Hey, Flagg, wait for baby! Aren't we all? The rest is silence. It only seems like never." It is needless to say that these lines do not get you anywhere; but, as I said before, I never was really going anywhere.

There was this pretty girl fixing the typewriter, and because it was early on a lovely October day, and I felt cheerful, I wrote Elliott Nugent as follows: "You and I are going to write a play together." His reply was prompt and to the point: "No, we're not." So I went out to Hollywood and showed him the typewriter scene, and he sighed and sat down, and began cutting it out. The collaboration was on.

After you have worked on nothing but dialogue for five months, you wonder if you can ever learn to write straight English prose again, the kind that comes in paragraphs and looks so nice. At first you are scared to try it, but finally you realize you have to, so you sit down, and, for practice, just to get back into the swing of the thing, you try to set down Lincoln's Gettysburg address. What comes out is this:

Four score and seven years ago, our fathers brought forth . . .
Your fathers! Always your fathers!
I said ours.
You meant yours!
. . . on this continent, a new nation, conceived in liberty . . .
I know! I know! And delegated to the proposition . . .
Not delegated! Dedicated!
. . . that all men are created equal.
ELLEN [*bitterly*]: All men are created equal! That sounds fine coming from you!
Enter JOE
"What's the matter with that tall thin man at the typewriter, mamma?"
"Hush, child, he's going crazy."

JAMES THURBER

Thurber Reports His Own Play,
The Male Animal,
with His Own Cartoons

This Thurber cartoon shows no particular scene but gives general idea of the prevailing bedlam. Dazed man at right is producer Herman Shumlin.

EDITOR'S NOTE: *Life* magazine asked Thurber for these seven illustrations for their January 29, 1940, issue. Written with Elliott Nugent, who also starred as the Midwestern English teacher in this canonical battle of the sexes, *The Male Animal* enjoyed an enormous success on Broadway, playing for 243 performances in the 1939–1940 season.

Husband is deeply hurt when he comes downstairs to see his wife dancing with an ex–football hero who once made love to her. He accuses them of dancing "like angels," says she never danced so blissfully with him.

Wife bolts upstairs sobbing and screaming at her husband's accusation. The two men confront each other angrily, then both begin to feel scared at the wife's outburst and wonder who should go upstairs to soothe her.

JAMES THURBER

Husband gets drunk at home while wife goes to football game with ex–football hero. Here with his friend he resolves to fight for his wife like all the other male animals which he pictures in the cloud above him.

The big fight, drawn in Thurber's best madhouse style, begins when the drunken husband socks the ex–football player on the nose. The male animals scuffle ineffectively while the females scream with excitement.

After the fight, wife stands between her two warriors and announces dramatically she is going to live in sin with the ex–football player. He is horrified by this news because he wants to go back to his own wife.

Husband dances with wife in this final scene of reconciliation, as the ex–football player gladly ducks out, and the ubiquitous Thurber dog, who was not in the play, casts a baleful eye over the happy ending.

JAMES THURBER

The Quality of Mirth

In the American theatre, or what is left of it, the quality of mirth is strained through many divergent judgments, each of them handed down with the air and tone of final authority that we Americans assume so easily.

"Who knows what's funny?" W. C. Fields used to say, meaning that all those around him were positive they knew, but intimating the real truth, that Fields was the final authority. When a producer or a director or a supervisor once came to him in Hollywood, laughing like crazy, and told him about a wonderful gagerino on a switcheroo, again he said, grimly, "Who knows what's funny?" Their idea had been that Fields would be rowing this boat—see—and suddenly the oars break in two. "The oars don't break," the great man said. "The oars bend." And in the movie they did bend, like leaden spoons, for Fields had been able to convince the multiple experts on comedy that he was right.

Surely no other American institution is so bound around and tightened up by rules, strictures, adages, and superstitions as the Broadway theatre. I have been mixed up in it (and I use that verb deliberately) off and on for quite a while. Long enough, anyway, to appreciate Jimmy Durante's "Everybody wants to get into the act."

There are those who are arrogant about their profound knowledge of comic effects and their long study and practice of the art of laughter, but for the most part people genuinely want to help, and are earnest in their efforts to "save the show" or "fix up that snapper at the end" or tell you what to take out or put in. Some of these specialists in humor were not even born the year I went to work for

The New Yorker, but, at 65, I have learned that it is a good idea to listen. In the first place, at least one out of every twelve suggestions is sound and, in the second place, the suggesters have increased my knowledge of the nature of the American male and female in our time.

We all know that the theatre and every play that comes to Broadway have within themselves, like the human being, the seed of self-destruction and the certainty of death. The thing is to see how long the theatre, the play, and the human being can last in spite of themselves. The biggest problem of all three is to preserve honorable laughter in a comedy. If a playwright tried to see eye to eye with everybody, he would get the worst case of strabismus since Hannibal lost an eye trying to count his nineteen elephants during a snowstorm while crossing the Alps.

Among the hundreds of adages that both help and hamper the theatre, one of the most persistent is "Only the audience knows," or "Only the audience can tell you." This is certainly true, but, in the case of a comedy, it is necessary to understand the quality of mirth in an audience.

We are a nation that has always gone in for the loud laugh, the wow, the yak, the belly laugh, and the dozen other labels for the roll-'em-in-the-aisles gagerissimo. This is the kind of laugh that delights actors, directors, and producers, but dismays writers of comedy because it is the laugh that often dies in the lobby. The appreciative smile, the chuckle, the soundless mirth, so important to the success of comedy, cannot be understood unless one sits among the audience and feels the warmth created by the quality of laughter that the audience takes home with it.

This failure of discrimination on the part of so many panicky and high-strung theatre people accounts, more than anything else, for the deplorable decline of stage comedy during the last decade. "Louder and funnier" should often read "louder, but less funny." There is a kind of mirth that brings forth a general audience sound a little like sighing, just as there is a kind of mirth that, in the true appreciator of it, can cause the welling up of tears.

This last phenomenon happened to me, as I once reported on this page, during the wonderful "Rain in Spain" scene in *My Fair Lady,*

JAMES THURBER

in which comedy, song, dance, characterization, and progress of plot were all beautifully conjoined.

The pre-Broadway road tour of a play is known as a "shake-down," but a better name would be "shape-up." The first term suggests shaking the holy bejudas out of it, while the second implies an effort at perfecting the "property," as lawyers always call a play. Lawyers now have a great hand in the shakedown, I have discovered, for contracts and contract clauses are waved at one as frequently as suggested gags. Howard Dietz once said, "A day away from Tallulah is like a month in the country," which brought out of me one night, on the road with *Carnival,* this thought: "Seven weeks on the road with a play is like ten years with Harold Ross."

Beginning in 1921 with the road company of an Ohio State musical comedy club called "Scarlet Mask," I have collected a vast amount of advice on how to write humor and comedy. I had written, thirty-nine years ago, the book for a musical show called *O My Omar!* and everybody then living in Cleveland, Cincinnati, and Dayton told me how it should have been done.

Since then I have been told, among other things: "You can't bring a play to Broadway entitled *The Male Animal,*" "You can't have a serious villain in a comedy," and "You've got to keep too much charm out of a comedy." The soundest critic of *The Male Animal* was Groucho Marx, who said, in Hollywood, "You got too many laughs in it. Take some of them out." He meant we should take out irrelevant gags and stick to the laughter of character and situation, and he was, of course, right.

When I tell this to the eminent authorities on comedy in our declining comic theatre, they yell, "Take laughs out of a comedy? That's crazy. Keep putting more laughs in." It means nothing to these experts that two of the biggest laughs in *The Male Animal* came on these two lines: "I felt fine" and "Yes, you are." This brings us to what I call the Fourth Strike.

The Fourth Strike grows out of the neurotic or just thoughtless conviction of many theatre people that if a line does not get a yell it isn't getting a thing. Let me give an example of the Fourth Strike. One night, on the shakedown, in a fable that has since been eliminated from the show, the line "A thing of beauty is a joy for such a little time" was inadvertently spoken this way, "A thing of joy is a beauty for such a little time." At least six friends of mine, or total strangers, shouted, "Keep it in!"

I have most resented the application to what I write of such adjectives as "mild," "gentle," "pixie," and "zany." Having tried for four decades to make some social comment, it is something less than reassuring to discover that what a jittery America wants is the boppo laugh or nothing. In the section of this revue which deals with "The Pet Department," it has been assumed by practically everybody that this is sheer nonsense. What I had in mind, along with laughter, was a sharp comment on one of the worst faults of Americans of both sexes, a hasty and thoughtless lack of observation and perception, and I have tried to present this by showing, with the use of symbols, that we often cannot tell a bear from a St. Bernard, a seagull from a rabbit, or a live dog from a cast-iron lawn dog.

All through this road trip the item known as "The Owl in the Attic" has been put in and taken out and put back. I hope it will be in the play when it opens in New York, if only as a tribute to Robert Benchley, who must have been told by 10,000 people during his lifetime how to write and present comedy. He once wrote me, "I don't laugh out loud very much, any more than you do, but I did at your line, 'This is the only stuffed bird I ever saw with its eyes closed, but whoever had it stuffed probably wanted it stuffed that way.' " On stage, this does not get a belly laugh or wow; in fact, I have been told, thirty times, "It doesn't get a thing."

It got a thing for the late Robert Benchley, so, again, I hope it stays in the revue. It is, I suppose, possible, since anything in present-day America is possible, that theatre people and audiences knew more about comedy than Benchley, Perelman, De Vries, Sullivan, White, and little old me, but I shall have to wait and find out. If they are right and we are wrong, I shall return to the dignity of the printed page, where it may be that I belong.

JAMES THURBER

The World Laughs with Them

THURBER
ON THE STATE OF HUMOR

And the World
Laughs with Them

The *New York Sunday Times,* which keeps me in touch with the progress of everything, printed an article recently entitled, with elegant inversion, "Furiously Proceeds Radio's Gag Hunt." "Luckily," says the author of the article, at the outset, "every joke can be twisted; some of them 1,000 times." I think that is a purely American exaggeration (we always seem to exaggerate more than anybody else). I do not believe that any joke can be twisted a thousand times. For more than two hours, after reading the story, I tried twisting old jokes, beginning with "Who was that lady I seen you with last night?" "That was no lady, that was my wife." To my surprise, all that I had when I counted up was twenty-seven twists, none of which was terribly funny; most of them were pretty labored, such as, "Who was that knight I seen you with last, lady?" "That was no knight, that was my husband." The thing that surprised me was that I could have sworn I had at least seventy or eighty different twists, instead of only twenty-seven. I think that after you have twisted a joke twenty-seven times it must always seem like about seventy or eighty times, and I should imagine that if you heard a joke being twisted by somebody else, instead of twisting it yourself, the total would seem even higher. It was probably this illusion of multiplicity which led the *Times* writer to make the statement that some jokes could be twisted a thousand times. Of course, he pointed out that the crack brains of Radio, the star gagmen, have a clever technique of their own, which you and I don't know anything about, for reworking old jokes. They have to have, because a joke can be told over the radio only once, the author says; after that it has to be twisted if you use it again. A joke that can be twisted a thousand times, or rather a gagman that can twist one a thousand times, is therefore extremely important to Radio. Take an expert who thinks up gags for a program that is broadcast three times a week—roughly, a hundred and fifty times a year. He could rework, for seven solid years, a joke that was used on the very first program. Most of us, even if we knew the technique, would go crazy long before we reached the second year. Radio gagmen do not go crazy. They always have before them the shining ambition of setting new world's records in writing wisecracks, and this keeps them mentally fit and alert. Let one of them hear that a rival gagman has written 28,000 words of funny dialogue in one night, and he will sit down and try to write 30,000 in one night. What is more, he will probably do it. Let one of them hear that a rival has twisted a joke—say the mother-in-law joke—1,098 times, and he will try to reach 1,100. This furious competition is a boon to Radio and is the reason that Radio is more important than the periodical. Nobody who works for a magazine has the energy or the enthusiasm to try to outdo anybody else, and as a result Radio gets off more than four thousand times as many gags every week as all the weekly magazines in the country put together.

Not content with twisting just one joke, I went on to experiment with some favorites of mine, starting with the lines from the play *The First Year* in which the lady says to her colored cook, "Did you seed the grapefruit?" and the cook answers, "Yes'm, Ah seed it." I couldn't get any twists to that at all, and it was pretty humiliating to realize that any one of seven hundred gagmen could have walked into the room and twisted it eight or ten times while I was mixing him a drink. Then, in a last attempt, I took Fred Allen's line about the scarecrow that scared some crows so badly they brought back corn they had stolen two years before. I didn't do so well with that one, either. For one thing, I am not sure of the rules; I don't know exactly what constitutes a new twist, but I should think it would not be fair to change the two years to three years (and so on up) or to change the crows to sharks or mongeese or any other creature that does not normally steal corn. What I tried to get in my twists was something scaring something so badly it would bring back something it had, quite in the natural course of its habits, stolen. It was too much for me. I began with a beekeeper scaring bears so badly they brought back honey they had stolen, but that didn't work because bears do not carry honey away with them; they eat it right at the hive, or the comb. I next tried scaring the beekeeper and then the bees, but both of those ideas became *too* twisted. If you have a bear scaring a bee-keeper so badly that the beekeeper gives the bear honey that the beekeeper has been trying to keep away from the bear, that is a basically funny idea, but the story, in the telling, falls down of its own weight. There is too much explaining to be done; the thing loses the clearcut quality and the sharply defined point of the original crow story. I have no doubt that any gagman could straighten me out, but I don't want to be straightened out. I want to go along through life believing that there aren't any twists to the crow story worth making. I know, of course, that if everybody believed the way I do, Radio would go out of business in a week. But that's the way I want to go along through life, anyway.

The *Times* article went on to a consideration of the "two great reservoirs" of humor. The first is the mistakes that children make. Many "gems of humor that have rocked the house" have come out of these mistakes. The article cites one about a little child that came to its father with a newspaper and said that they'd have to hurry to the World's Fair, because it was only going to last two days. The father said no, that the Fair was going to last all year, whereupon the child showed him a line in the paper reading "Fair today and tomorrow." Thousands of such lines are taken over as their own by adult comedians every year. The second great reservoir consists of the "errors of foreigners who cripple and garble the language." Take the gagman's landlord, who was a foreigner and who said to the gagman one day (according to the *Times*), "I'll give you one of two choices: either get out or move." And who, on another occasion, when his tenant was complaining about the lights, said, "They're all right, they're 60-wops." Unknowingly, says the article, the landlord sup-plied much comedy for the coast-to-coast audience of America. It seems that everything this landlord said was funny.

Not all gagmen, of course, have children and foreigners to fall back on, but there are always the seven basic forms of jokes. The *Times* author went around asking various gagmen about these. The answer of one of them, Mr. Carroll Carroll, is interesting. "I suppose one [of the seven basic forms] is that 'anything out of place is funny,' " said Mr. Carroll. "For example, false teeth in the pocket or on a table are funnier than in the mouth." With a rule like that to go by, Radio gagmen have, of course, another practically inexhaustible reservoir. They can speak of crutches in a coffin, or wooden legs in a bed of roses. All such incongruities are ludicrous and serve to keep the coast-to-coast audience in stitches from day to day. Here again the Radio writers seem to me to be worlds ahead of the magazine writers because, although it is much harder to get over a story on the radio about false teeth on a table than it is to tell it in a magazine, there have been in the past year over three thousand more false-teeth jokes on the air than in the prints. Once more the Radio gagman's enormous gusto and tireless energy win out over the pallid, lackadaisical nature of the magazine writer. And yet consider what the gagman is up against! If he is doing a sketch about the finding of a set of false teeth on a table, he has to have somebody come into the room (the studio broadcasting-room) and say, "Why, what is that lying there on the table?" and somebody else has to say, "What? I don't see anything." "Why, yes you do—there on the table." The first speaker then goes over and picks up the false teeth and drops them back on the table. "Why, they're false teeth!" he giggles. Now, the sound of false teeth dropping on a table is a very difficult sound to produce through a microphone. If you actually dropped a pair of false teeth on a table, it would sound like dropping a heavy glass paper-clip holder or a fragment of broken inkwell. The proper effect is gained by dropping two cigar-box lids which have been lightly glued together. It is not very easy to laugh at that, and therefore the actor who picks up and drops the lids must imagine that he is actually picking up and dropping a set of false teeth. In a magazine story, the whole thing could be accomplished much more simply: "There was a set of false teeth lying on the table. Romley looked at them for a moment, then he burst out laughing." And yet, as I say, the Radio gagmen never flinch or falter. They think up such things as finding a glass eye in a robin's nest and they write it out and the comedians put it on the air and the coast-to-coast audience rocks with laughter. It makes a magazine writer feel as if there were simply no reason to go on any longer.

JAMES THURBER

"He gave up smoking and humor the first of the year."

"There is no laughter in this house."

JAMES THURBER

Groucho and Me

More than twenty years ago my wife and I were entertained at dinner in London by an American diplomat and his wife. It was black tie, of course, and I had steeled myself for an evening of polite conversation. Instead, our host took us to see the smartest show in town and the hardest to get into, the Marx Brothers' *A Day at the Races.* Two years later, in Hollywood, I met the protean author of *Groucho and Me,* and I'll be darned if we were not, within five minutes, engaged in a serious discussion of Henry James's ghost story "The Jolly Corner."

There is nothing ghostly or ghosted about *Groucho and Me.* The "Me" is a comparatively unknown Marx named Julius Henry Marx. Groucho and Julius are one, but not the same. The latter is a writer from away back. When *The New Yorker* was six weeks old, in April 1925, it printed the first of four short casuals that year, signed Julius H. Marx. In 1929 there were three more pieces in the magazine, this time signed Groucho Marx. I think Harold Ross had insisted that Groucho come out from behind his real name and admit, you might say, who he wasn't.

Julius-Groucho's *New Yorker* pieces consisted of anecdotes, dialogues, jokes, and reminiscences. They dealt with vaudeville, Boston, the Middle West, and press agents, and there was one entitled "Buy It, Put It Away, and Forget About It." It appeared in May 1929 and began like this: "I come from common stock. I always planned to begin my autobiography with this terse statement. Now that introduction is out. Common stock made a bum out of me."

This is the way the autobiography of Julius H. Marx actually begins: "The trouble with writing a book about yourself is that you can't fool around. If you write about some one else, you can stretch the truth from here to Finland. If you write about yourself, the slightest deviation makes you realize instantly that there may be honor among thieves, but *you* are just a dirty liar." Julius often cuffs himself about like that, and he takes Groucho in his stride. You learn about the comedian almost incidentally, for the book turns its brightest spotlight on the humorist, wit, essayist, philosopher, and man of many worlds.

The twenty-eight chapters are, in part, a saga of the five sons of a Yorkville tailor and his wife, and of how they came out of the Nowhere into the Here, out of the small time into the big time, out of a dark obscurity and into a luminous fame. Well, there *was* one spark of immortality in the family to begin with. A maternal uncle of the Marx boys was Mr. Shean, who rode to undying fame in the company of Mr. Gallagher.

In the song "Fine and Dandy" there is a line that goes, "Even trouble has its funny side," but Groucho, as I shall call him from now on, shows not only the funny side of trouble, but also the troublesome side of fun. Before the Marx Brothers became an everlasting part of our great comedic history and tradition, they ran the hard gamut of everything. The purely autobiographical chapters, in the swift, ex-

Harpo

Groucho

Chico

JAMES THURBER

pert, and uniquely witty style of the master, tell how the young Marxes—Chico, the eldest, was the only one to graduate from grammar school—survived the abuses, loneliness, crookedness, and cruelty of small-time vaudeville without becoming disenchanted by show business, although they had to fight for a livelihood, learned to carry blackjacks, and to hold their own with the monsters called theatre managers. The only hospitality they enjoyed in the awful early years on the road was supplied by sporting houses and pool rooms, for the actor was suspect, not glamorous, in those days.

Groucho's book might have been subtitled "How I Ran an Allowance of Five Cents a Week into an Income of $18,000 a Week, with a Vicuña Coat and Two Cadillacs Thrown In." Money plays a big part in this, as in any other American success story, and in a chapter called "How I Starred in the Follies of 1929" he tells how he lost nearly a quarter of a million in the stock market crash. (That May 1929 *New Yorker* piece of his was indeed prophetic.)

The stock market did not make bums out of the Marxes. It was a kind of godsend, for in 1931 they went to Hollywood where their guardian angel introduced them to Irving Thalberg, the man responsible for the screening of *A Day at the Races* and that finest of all Marx masterpieces, *A Night at the Opera.* The book gleams and glitters with the names of show business and show art. George Kaufman is praised for his valuable contribution to the Marx success, and we meet, or rather Groucho met, Charlie Chaplin when the Little Man was making only fifty bucks a week in an act called "A Night at the Club."

Everything in the book is fresh and new, for neither Julius nor Groucho included any of his earlier writings. Those two share a cold eye, a warm heart, and a quick perception. *Groucho and Me* is an important contribution to the history of show business and to the saga of American comedy and comedians, comics and comicality.

JAMES THURBER PRESENTS
Der Tag aux Courses

The gentlemen pictured on the opposite page were, as everybody knows, the central figures in *Das Duck Soup* and other things of the sort, and are not to be confused with—or even by, as far as that goes—the author of *Das*

Kapital, who wore a beard and looked a little like Sanity Clause (Karl Marx, 1818–1883). The Marx Brothers (1776–2937) are not, as a matter of fact, to be confused by anybody. You may remember that on one occasion when a suspicious plainclothes man, observing that, whereas only two Marxes were seated at a certain breakfast table, there were nevertheless covers laid for twice as many, said sharply, "This table is set for four," Groucho, in no wise confused, replied, "That's nothing, the alarm clock is set for eight." If nothing else set off the Marx Brothers from Karl Marx that would. Karl Marx had the sort of mind which, faced with the suggestion that the stolen painting was hidden in the house next door, would, on learning that there *was* no house next door, never have thought to build one. Here is where, again, he parts company with the Marx Brothers. The significance of this divergence becomes clear when it is known that the Marx Brothers recovered the painting. If that is a horse below, and if it isn't we'll build one, it is one of a number of objects that help litter up the forthcoming Marx Brothers picture, *A Day at the Races (Der Tag aux Courses).*

JAMES THURBER

Speaking of Humor . . .

You have to enjoy humorous writing while you're doing it. Anybody who says he doesn't is lying (he may, of course, not like to start). You've got to be enjoying it. You can't be mad, or bitter, or irate. If you are it will be no good. . . . The things we laugh at are awful while they are going on, but get funny when we look back. And other people laugh because they've been through it too. The closest thing to humor is tragedy.

My English teacher at Ohio State, Herman A. Miller, told me of something he saw which illustrates this.

One gray and snowy Sunday morning, about 10 o'clock, a small-ish husband leading a little fluffy dog on a leash went into a delicatessen store to buy food. Herman said he looked like the cartoon of the Common People in the conventional political caricature. Well, his wife had given him a formidable list of things to buy, so that when he came out of the store both arms were laden with butter, bread, eggs, oranges, etc. It was a problem to handle the dog and the bundles both. Finally, the dog made a lunge and broke away. The man stood there juggling his bundles, dropping one, picking it up, dropping another, calling "Here doggie, here doggie" all the time; then finally setting out onto the icy street, gingerly, in pursuit of the dog. Before he got to it a car rounded a corner and struck the dog and killed it. The little man just stood there blinking, holding his bundles. That was the highest point of sadness in the scene, all right.

EDITOR'S NOTE: For the source of each interview or article, please see the Notes on page 259, matching the key word at the end of each excerpt with the list's respective entry.

But then, still bewildered, always the husband who had to get the groceries home, he tried to pick the dog up and still hold the bundles. After dropping the butter and bread he had to drop the dog again to pick them up. In this amazing moment there was that almost crazy laugh, for here, so closely joined as to be almost incredible, was pathos and slapstick. Herman used to relate that story to his class and ask their opinion of whether it was funny, sad, horrible, or what. And why.

I think humor is the best that lies closest to the familiar, to that part of the familiar which is humiliating, distressing, even tragic. Humor is a kind of emotional chaos told about calmly and quietly in retrospect. There is always a laugh in the utterly familiar. If a play is going on on the stage, a love scene, say, and from the wings a Scotty should wander on, with muddy paws, having got away from its owner's dressing room, and if the Scotty should jump up on the best sofa and lie down, it would be funnier than if a kangaroo popped in. There'd be a laugh at the kangaroo, too. The laughers would think "that poor sap!" (of the man in the love scene). There you'd have your sense of superiority in a laugh. In the case of the Scotty, however, the laughers would say, "Just what Rowdy did when the Smiths called that time." This is my way, anyway, I think. People can laugh out of a kind of mellowed self-pity as well as out of superiority.

Human dignity, the humorist believes, is not only silly but a little sad. So are dreams and conventions and illusions. The fine brave fragile stuff that men live by. They look so swell, and go to pieces so easily.

You know that hysterical laugh that people sometimes get in the face of the Awful. Maybe it's the rockbottom of humor. Anyway it exists. [EASTMAN]

*   *   *

"Waterville"
Paget East, Bermuda
June 9, 1954
Dear Mr. Landau:

You may have a point in what you say about the effect of humor on Stevenson's defeat, but after all the score against him was only 33 to

JAMES THURBER

27. If we have to have Zeitgeist in the case of humor, *Time* magazine may be right in indicating that humor is a diminishing thing. One of its primary elements is the unexpected, and if people have to be all prepared for that, they might be let down a little. I think Louis Kronenberger is right when he says that Americans do not have a basic humorous sense, but are rather more jolly and open-hearted than humorous. In such a nation humor is always a little suspect, but so are modern music and painting and anything intellectual.

The subject of children and humor is one of the hardest I can think of. It often lies close to the grisly for them. Not many adults have the kind of total recall that lets them remember what was funny to them as children. In the many letters I have got from children, usually about my fairy tales, they rarely pick out anything funny as having interested them. They seem to like the weird and the grotesque more, and to pick out strange or colorful characters as such, rarely mentioning anything these characters say. The humor of action seems to be their favorite type. I often wonder what the average child would think of *The Innocent Voyage.* Kids also seem to be amused by any kind of accident at all, no matter how gory its results. All this shows up in the trend toward horror that began so long ago in the comic books, which I understand are no longer comic at all.

These are merely offhand comments on a subject I have often intended to go into more deeply. . . .

Cordially yours,

JAMES THURBER

P.S. When my own daughter was about 6, she assured me one day that Munro Leaf was "the funniest writer." It seems she liked his series of books with such titles as *Arithmetic Can Be Fun,* or whatever they were. She also was more delighted when I talked bad French or German to her, than by anything of mine in English, when she was 8 to 10. They all seem to love strange sounding words, alliterative sentences, and the like, whether they get the meaning of it or not. Also, there have been a great many times when I haven't had the vaguest idea of what the hell they were laughing about. They have a lot of secret areas of laughter, such as the giggles. I doubt that anything giggled about by children is actually very funny. [LANDAU]

West Cornwall
Connecticut
June 25, 1954
Dear Mr. Landau:

I read your letter again after I got home from Bermuda, because I had heard on radio a couple of brief references to humor that interested and surprised me. Mr. Welch, in his closing talk the last day of the famous hearings, said something about "getting back to humor," and on a public forum John Chamberlain . . . said that Cohn and Adams had been talking humor and not making threats in their original exchanges that caused all the trouble. Here again we find the idea, curious to me, of taking humor off and putting it on like a blazer or an overcoat. All this supports the contention of Kronenberger that our conception of humor is not deep-seated or basic. It seems to me that true humor should be an integral part of human nature, something like heart action or breathing. In some poem or other A. E. Housman has a line like this: "Straps on the sword that cannot save." If humor is something like a sword, maybe it has to be strapped on, but nobody should go around without it in any period of time. It is like imagination, one of the necessary accessories of fortitude. Since one of its chief constituents is taste, it should be used sparingly sometimes and left in its sheath at other times, but it should always be handy. This purely American idea of getting out of it and getting back to it seems to me fundamentally unhumorous and even antihumorous. Lincoln, as everybody knows, began all his Cabinet meetings during the Civil War with some joke, momentarily wiping the blood of the Antietam off the old sabre. Even then there were those who criticized him for levity during tragedy.

It was only a few years ago that some perceptive Englishman pointed out the basic silliness of Horatio Nelson's famous last words, "Kiss me, Hardy," and proved his conviction that what the dying man really said was, "Kismet, Hardy," that is to say, "This is it," or, as they say in Bermuda, "I've had my chocolate." Nobody had ever laughed before at the hilarious picture of a stern old sea-dog asking another stern old sea-dog to kiss him, so it all depends. . . .

Cordially yours,

JAMES THURBER

JAMES THURBER

P.S. It seems to me that Chamberlain and McCarthy are way off about humor and confuse it with kidding around, a coarse form of mental horseplay. Humor does not include sarcasm, invalid irony, sardonicism, innuendo, or any other form of cruelty. When these things are raised to a high point they can become wit, but unlike the French and English, we have not been much good at wit since the days of Benjamin Franklin. [LANDAU]

* * *

[In response to the idea of "cruel humor" Thurber counters:] I don't think that those two words can be used together. By definition, humor is gentle. The savage, the cruel, the harsh would fall under the heading of wit and/or satire, as the lawyers say. Now, my definitions are these: The wit makes fun of other persons; the satirist makes fun of the world; the humorist makes fun of himself, but in so doing, he identifies himself with people—that is, people everywhere, not for the purpose of taking them apart, but simply revealing their true nature. [SMALL WORLD]

* * *

Intoning is almost impossible in humor, which cannot afford the ornaments and indulgences of fine writing, the extravagance of consciousness-streaming, or lower case unpunctuation meanderings. There is a sound saying in the theatre: "You can't play comedy in the dark." I saw Jed Harris and Billy Rose trying to disprove this one night in Philadelphia twenty-five years ago when they put on an 8-minute Don Marquis skit in absolute darkness: the sounds of voices, glasses, and the cash register of an old-time beer saloon. People fell asleep, or began coughing, or counting their change, or whispering to their neighbors, or reading their programs with pencil flashlights. Comedy has to be done en clair. You can't blunt the edge of wit or the point of satire with obscurity. Try to imagine a famous witty saying that is not immediately clear. [COWLEY LETTER]

* * *

COLLECTING HIMSELF

The word "funny" has come to mean almost everything except just that. It can mean crazy, as in Funny House; peculiar, as in "She's funny that way"; ominous, as in "That's funny—they don't answer"; mysterious, as in the feminine "How do you make this do-funny work?"; stunned or silly, as in "Watch it, Mac, or I'll punch you funny"; and strange or terrible, as in "It's a funny world."

Art Buchwald, a prominent nonconformist, insists on being funny in the good old-fashioned way—that is, amusing, entertaining, and hilarious. In the various capitals of the world, ancient mariners and others stop me and say, "Is he a man or a myth?" To this I always say, "Just wait until you see him." When they see him, they know that he is a man, a lot of man, but that is oversimplification. He is a man with winged feet and winged words, who gets around the world in person and in prose, and his new book [*More Caviar*] proves that. It also proves that he is a sharp observer of his strange species and one of the best reporters now reporting. My own close investigation of Art Buchwald, as man and myth, has revealed that he is half Falstaff, half Hamlet, an Aw Shucks cosmopolite, a great big good-natured aesthete, a monastic gadabout, a loyal husband and devoted father, in spite of his striking resemblance to the late Rudolph Valentino and the magic spell he casts in the glittering salons and shady hide-outs of Paris, London, New York and other dangerous cities.

"Did you read Art Buchwald today?" has become as commonplace as the inevitable answer, "I certainly did." [BUCHWALD]

* * *

Humor isn't considered one of the major arts. . . . The best essay on humor I know was written by Andy White in *A Subtreasury of American Humor.* I guess books of humor don't last because, like the passions, humor is a changing thing. It is likely to date because it deals in the modern idiom. I wonder about *Babbitt,* whether the humor in that wouldn't date? According to Mencken, there are only two American novels, *Babbitt* and *Huck Finn.* The best estimate of my work was done by T. S. Eliot. . . . Most humorous books date and the serious books don't. When you see *As You Like It* you know it was written over 250 years ago. [Of *Tristram Shandy:*] I haven't tried those old books. I can't get through *Pickwick Papers.* And don't forget there's a cult around the old work which makes it difficult to know when it's

JAMES THURBER

funny and when it's supposed to be funny. I can't remember any humor in old Scott Fitzgerald. Humor would have saved him. It seems to me the great novelists have humor in them, even if it isn't predominent. The Russians had it; Gogol had it, and Dostoevsky. It seems to me Fitzgerald strangled humor because he was caught in the romantic tradition. Well, there isn't a trace of humor in Communism, is there? I think any political system that vehemently attacks humor reveals a great weakness. It is one of the dangers universally. One of the great things we have here is humor—even in war. We ought not to lose that. [BREIT-2]

* * *

When *Life* called me "mild" in 1945 my old friend Nunnally Johnson said, "It must be a misprint for 'wild.' " Boris Karloff is mild but I am not. Other mild guys are James Cagney and Peter Lorre unless backed into a corner. I am in a corner without being backed there and often come out fighting. [LIFE]

* * *

A certain professor of English in America has written a dissertation on my work, in which he speaks of my "major phase" as if it were in the past. If it is in the past, I shall demote it from major to sergeant, for a man's major phases, whether he be a writer or President of the United States, should be ahead of him, and not behind him. [TIME]

JAMES THURBER

The State of Humor
in the States

Is there a national sense of humor, or does it vary regionally, like accents, climate, idioms, crops, and politics? I am not peering at you over professorial spectacles, class, but merely reporting a question often asked me since "A What's-his-name Carnival" took to the road last January to play Columbus, Detroit, Cleveland, St. Louis, Cincinnati, Pittsburgh, New York, and Central City, Colorado, the famous town up mountain a piece from Denver. The question calls for careful investigation, perhaps by a Congressional subcommittee, since humor, as we all know, is American, and its disappearance would therefore be un-American, but I'll take a unilateral swing at it, anyway.

First of all, the restless flux and shift of considerable portions of our population has brought to each of these cities to live many former residents of all the others. In Denver one hears as often as in New York, "Oh, but I wasn't born here." There are in Denver a hundred and fifty graduates and former students of my own university, Ohio State. I should say that humor, such as it is today, is national with, of course, regional and local variants. Any nationalistic phenomenon is possible in a country in which the famous Giants and the immortal Dodgers now represent, respectively, San Francisco and Los Angeles.

If we are in a period of decadence—that is, retrogression in literature and art—as I believe we are, then comedy, being literature and one of the arts, is bound to have declined, and indeed it has. During the dark decade now coming happily to a close, it took, as every thinking person knows, a beating from both the far Left and the far Right. Let me report at once, however, that I have been cheered by signs of its coming revival, for humor is innate and resilient. If I may brag a little (and I shall, whether I may or not), *Carnival* broke a twenty-nine-year-old record for the opera house in Central City by selling out completely for the month of August before it opened. Not only that, but three extra performances had to be put on. It is true that Mae West in *Diamond Lil* also sold out in advance, many years ago, but its run was much shorter and tickets cost far less. It was heartening to hear Americans laughing again at my occasional kidding of the faults and foibles of Congress and government, but then, it is only fair to say, I had heard the same hearty laughter at the line "You can't quarantine a congressman" in *Teahouse of the August Moon* and the repeated "the goddam Senate" in *The Solid Gold Cadillac.* This may mean that more people than I had hoped read Elmer Davis's *But We Were Born Free,* which featured that great and valiant American's injunction to us all, "Don't let them scare you."

There is still some timidity and confusion of thought ("anemia of thought," Professor Ernest Hocking has called it), for two lines of mine in what we call the Word Dances caused a nervous flutter here and there. One of these was "Do you know the difference between free speech and loose talk?" The other one, seriously intended to jostle our complacent ignorance of true Americanism, was "Why do we have to have a secret ballot? It sounds so underhanded." That line, I just now realize, is no longer in the play. Senator McCarthy did indeed make it hard for us to tell the difference between the patriotic and the subversive.

Anyone who travels, with stopovers, between New York and Denver is likely to be disturbed, or even alarmed, by our national disdain for the processes of intellect. In almost every city I heard the word "intellectual" identified with "literary" and "sophisticated." Too many persons seem surprised that the humor and comedy in the play is simple, clear, and understandable, and yet without those qualities there can be no humor or comedy. "Why, it isn't too subtle at all!" one woman told me at a party. "Even my daughter understood all of it!" And another lady exclaimed, "Why, I thought it would be highbrow and recondite!" This, I must confess, bewildered me, for the long history of *New Yorker* humor is scarcely one of oblique and abstruse approach to laughter. Among those who have written simple declarative sentences and pointed humor for *The New Yorker* are Robert Benchley, E. B. White, S. J. Perelman, Dorothy Parker, Frank Sullivan, and Wolcott Gibbs. Two of these, to be sure, are dead, and the others are heard from rarely, and this may have confused hasty and anemic readers. Humor has declined, God knows, in quantity, but its nature remains unchanged.

One thing that has changed since my newspaper days in Ohio, thirty-five to forty years ago, is the attitude west of the Alleghenies toward New York City. It used to be downright dislike, with more than a trace of inferiority complex, but now our great city is lightly patronized as a provincial town. Recently John Wayne put on a sneak preview of his new movie in Denver and was quoted in that city's press as saying, "California is too professional, and New York is too provincial." I remember when Al Smith was the figure and symbol of all that the Middle West disliked and distrusted about New York. And I remember a day in the early Twenties when I watched a traffic cop in Columbus motion the driver of a car to pull over to the curb. I was talking to the cop at the time and I asked him what the driver had done. "He's got New York license plates, hasn't he?" the cop said. "Let him cool off a while there. Those New York guys are too cocky."

In view of this, it surprised and pleased me, at a performance of *Sunrise at Campobello* in Denver two weeks ago, to hear the warm and delighted reception the audience gave to the actor playing the part of Al Smith, as well as its all-out appreciation of Whitfield Connor's excellent portrayal of F.D.R. "I wish," said a woman behind me, "they would have let Al say, 'raddio,' the way he always did." Roosevelt's eloquent attack on religious bigotry in politics was, by the way, loudly applauded.

Many things astonished, and sometimes bewildered, all of us on the road. There was the lady in Pittsburgh who said to me between acts, "Of course I like it, but your play is much too sophisticated for New York." And there was, even in Denver to my amazement, a general unfamiliarity with the name and achievements of Harold W. Ross, who was born in Aspen, Colorado, visited the state almost every year after he founded *The New Yorker,* and whose ashes were scattered by two army airplane pilots near his birthplace. One night I took part, over radio station KOA in Denver, in a panel discussion of this and that which lasted an hour and a half. This program invites phone calls, and listeners asked me to tell about E. B. White, Sid Perelman, and Dorothy Parker, but, I am grieved to say, not Harold Ross, although I kept referring to him as "the boy from Aspen."

So far as I know, there has never been a careful and extensive analysis of American theatre audiences. The findings of such a survey would constitute an important sociological document. A question-naire might be handed to those attending plays everywhere, asking them, among other things, where they come from, what they liked and didn't like, and why. A separate survey might well deal with the quality of audience laughter, but that would be hard because there are a dozen different kinds, from the inner and inaudible to the guffaw, taking in such variants as the laughter of shock, embarrass-ment, and, you might say, she-laughed-and-so-I-laughed-too, and even he-laughed-and-so-I-didn't. There is also the warm continuous laughter of recognition which Paul Ford, for example, always gets along with the laughter aroused by his skill and artistry. People on trains and at parties in every city called him Colonel Hall because of his fame as the commanding officer in the "Sergeant Bilko" television show. (The same kind of reception is also given to Peggy Cass.)

An important third survey, and a real toughy, would examine the varying reactions of actors to the feel or sense of the audience when the curtain goes up. The performer who puts himself inside a charac-ter, instead of allowing the character to disappear inside him, often seems as unaware of the audience as an artist painting a cathedral seems unaware of a crowd in the street watching him work. Then there is the performer, both male and female, upon whom the audi-ence acts as a powerful stimulant—say, five dry martinis—and who, consciously or unconsciously, multiplies his personality and his comic technique by three, or even five. His, or her, case merits the attention not only of critics, but of psychologists.

My own theatrical and literary allegiance is to that provincial town, New York City, U.S.A., whose drama critics were kind enough to detect the meaningful, the serious, and even the mordant beneath the comedy. West of the Alleghenies my humor was variously de-scribed as zany, pixie, wispy, quaint, not hip, old-fashioned, and elfin (I have challenged the man who used that word to a duel at ten paces with cold potato cakes).

In conclusion, a charming young lady at a garden party in Denver assured me that Edgar Allan Poe and Hemingway are intellectual, and therefore hard to understand. I asked her to name a non-intellectual who was easy to understand, and she said, "Why, W. Somerset Maugham." You take it from there, gentle reader. After all, the American scene, from the standpoint of humor, is too much for an aging pixie to handle by himself.

JAMES THURBER

How to Tell Government
from Show Business

History is replete with proofs, from Cato the Elder to Kennedy the Younger, that if you scratch a statesman you find an actor, but it is becoming harder and harder, in our time, to tell government from show business. The Congress of the United States, for many years now, has staged, rather than conducted, its sub-committee investigations, turning them into veritable television plays, starring various Senators and Congressmen. During the probe of the so-called Hollywood Ten, some years ago, at least one scene was actually rehearsed in advance, the way a drama is rehearsed in the theatre. A famous movie actor, whom I shall call the Friendly Witness, said, on the stand when the curtain went up, "There is one name that is never heard at a meeting of Hollywood Reds."

"What name is that?" a rehearsed Congressman demanded.

"God," said the Friendly Witness.

Congressional procedures reached the high-water mark of show business, of course, when that great ham, Joseph McCarthy, was starred in a series of television plays that might have been called "The War Against the Army." At that time, in my histrionic country, one Professor of Political Science deplored the bold and bald entrance of government into the area of show business, but the trend could not be stopped.

As if to fight back, or at least to hold its own, the Broadway theatre in recent years has staged plays dealing with government, such as *Sunrise at Campobello,* which starred Ralph Bellamy as Franklin

D. Roosevelt, *The Gang's All Here,* which starred Melvyn Douglas as Warren G. Harding, and *The Best Man,* in which more than one President or presidential aspirant was identifiable. Previously, we had had *The Patriots,* in which both George Washington and Thomas Jefferson appeared, but by far our best-known Broadway President is Raymond Massey, who played Abraham Lincoln more than once, so often, in fact, that the American playwright and wit, George Kaufman, said of him, "Massey won't be satisfied until he's assassinated."

This determined and continuing erasing of the line that once separated government and show business reached its most notable point during the last presidential campaign, when John F. Kennedy and Richard Nixon were co-starred in a series of television plays, mistakenly called debates. As everybody knows, the physical appearance, or make-up, of the two political actors, played at least as important a part in the shows as what they had to say. From now on, I think it is safe to predict, neither the Democratic nor the Republican Party will ever nominate for President a candidate without good looks, stage presence, theatrical delivery, and a sense of timing.

As a fond follower, or rather fan, of the new leading man in the White House, and his theatrically effective family, I am somewhat concerned about the choice of "The New Frontier" as the general title of the series of plays he is so dramatically staging in Washington. What is to prevent Senator Barry Goldwater of Arizona, a conservative opponent of the President's Party, and a man described by other men as handsome and by women as cute, from getting himself starred in a television Western called "The Old Frontier" and winning the audiences of America away from Caroline's father? If there is one fact about the United States that can be stated without fear of successful contradiction, it is that Americans, or the vast majority of Americans, are in love with the Far West, the Old Frontier.

There is much discussion in America at present about a proposed Federal, or National, theatre. It has stirred up great opposition, as any project called Federal or National is bound to do in a nation dedicated to free enterprise and States' rights. I think though that I see the way in which a compromise will finally be effected. Senators and Congressmen will demand, as a prerequisite to the establishment of a National theatre, the right to be cast in Broadway plays. It does not trouble me to imagine Adlai Stevenson playing Hamlet, but what does worry me is a recurring nightmare I have about the rewriting of certain plays of Shakespeare to fit the modern governmental scene. In the first of these bad dreams, I saw Lady Macbeth enter, not with a taper, but with a ballot box. From then on my fancies got out of hand, almost out of mind. I could hear a Senator declaiming, "To be elected or not to be elected, that is the question." I also heard the ugly paraphrase, "Out, out, brief candidate!" Everybody is having bad dreams nowanights, and I have no wish to make them worse, so I will cease all this wild imagining with one final bit of denigration of the Bard's lines: "Flights of voters sing thee to the White House."

The rest is silence.

On the Brink of Was

The twentieth century and I will be 70, Man willing, within six years of each other—I am the older—but the chances of either of us making it have been steadily reduced since the Wright brothers began fooling around with flying machines. The human being is the most self-destructive of animals, unless you count the Ed Wynn horse that kept banging into things, not because he was blind, but because he just didn't give a damn. The result has been that we are now living under the threat of total demolition on the Brink of Was. All this is having its effect upon every area of comedy, in England and on the continent, if not in America, which gives up the traditional more slowly than any other country.

The English theatre has been experimenting with what the *Times* of London calls "The Comedy of Menace." In a recent article, Mr. David Campton was named as one of the authors most closely connected with this type of comedy, and the writer comments, "Most of the Campton plays can be reduced to brief statements, such as politicians are dangerous half-wits."

I am afraid it is too soon after McCarthy for American playwrights to deal comically with such bold assumptions. During the past five months in England and France, the word I most often heard applied to American writing, including comedy, was "conformist," a polite way of saying "timid." Intelligent people among our European allies are still shocked and bewildered by the beating American writers and

EDITOR'S NOTE: This essay is Thurber's response to the following two questions posed by the *New York Times:* "Are we taking ourselves too seriously? Has satire on our private and public mores, as Will Rogers once practiced it, become unhealthfully scarce?"

JAMES THURBER

artists took during the McCarthy era. It is not expected that we will soon recover and contribute to a new and brave world literature of comedy.

The nation that complacently and fearfully allows its artists and writers to become suspected rather than respected is no longer regarded as a nation possessed with humor in depth. It is generally felt that a jumpy American—"afflicted with night terrors," as one London critic put it—has lost its right to leadership in the field of political satire. As a people, we have always preferred the gentle to the sharp, Will Rogers to Mencken, Finley Peter Dunne, William Allen White, and Elmer Davis.

Will Rogers was a skillful and lovable performer who held his audiences in the circle of his lariat by mild kidding and affable joshing of many close friends of his—Presidents, Cabinet members, Senators, Congressmen, and even state legislators. His was not the satire that comes from the heart by conviction, but the spoofing that comes from the top of the mind as a vaudeville routine. He deserves, but has never got, a competent biographer who could explode the myth and reveal the man.

The laughter of man is more terrible than his tears, and takes more forms—hollow, heartless, mirthless, maniacal. After the Comedy of Menace may comes the Comedy of Horror. The Lunts' vehicle, *The Visit,* comes close in places to the grisly whimsies of demonism. To a basically jolly people like us, lovers of tranquilizers in a perilous world, the New Comedy will come slowly, if ever, to the printed page. Even in the Twenties we had nobody who showed such promise in the area of the Comedy of Menace as Evelyn Waugh. We have the grisly, and even the ghastly, on all sides of us, but we are not apt to turn it into satire that would bring readers to books or audiences to theatres. And what would *The New Yorker* do if presented with such a drawing as this: "Please don't kill Mummy and Daddy tonight, Junior. It's our twelfth wedding anniversary"?

"Humor," said Lord Boothby the other day, "is the only solvent of terror and tensions." That is why the Communists have always discouraged humor. Their fixed grin, or Geneva smile, of three years ago, was as phony as a parrot's laugh. American must learn that humor, whatever form it may take, can be one of our strongest allies, but it cannot flourish in a weather of fear and hysteria and intimidation. Bravest of the brave in wartime, we are known abroad as the jumpiest of the jumpy in peacetime.

A few years ago, even wise men, who should have known better, were saying, "If Will Rogers were alive today, he would be put in jail." I keep telling my European friends that this is the sheerest nonsense. Will Rogers would have kidded around with the subcommittees of Congress as he once kidded around with Mussolini ("Dictator form of Government is the greatest form of Government there is, if you have the right Dictator. Well, these folks certainly have got him." That irresponsible observation was made by Mr. Rogers in *The Saturday Evening Post* in 1926, when nobody cared much about what anybody said).

Political satire can be as dangerous as an unguided missile when it is unsound. Political comedy must be grounded in serious knowledge of our nation and of the world. Perhaps Mort Sahl is the answer, or one of the answers. I have not yet heard him or his records. From what I have heard about him, he will not be intimidated.

Yes, Virginia, there is a bomb in Gilead, but don't just take another tranquilizer and walk the other way. Let's face it.

JAMES THURBER

"One more of these and I'll spill the beans about everybody here."

"He says he's just about got the government where he wants it."

At the crossroads.

Thinking Ourselves
into Trouble

Every man is occasionally visited by the suspicion that the planet on which he is riding is not really going anywhere; that the Force which controls its measured eccentricities hasn't got anything special in mind. If he broods on this somber theme long enough he gets the doleful idea that the laughing children on a merry-go-round or the thin, fine hands of a lady's watch are revolving more purposefully than he is. These black doubts creep up on a man just before thunderstorms or at six in the morning when the steam begins to knock solemnly in the pipes or during his confused wanderings in the forest beyond Euphoria after a long night of drinking.

Where are we going, if anywhere, and why?

It will do no good to call up the *Times* or consult the *Britannica.* The Answer does not lie in the charts of astronomers or in the equations of mathematicians; it was not indicated by Galileo's swinging lamp or the voices of Joan of Arc; it evaded Socrates and Archimedes and the great men of the Renaissance and everybody else from Francis Bacon to John Kieran.

The fearful mystery that lies behind all this endless rotation has led Man into curious indulgences and singular practices, among them love, poetry, intoxicants, religion, and philosophy. Philosophy offers the rather cold consolation that perhaps we and our planet do not actually exist; religion presents the contradictory and scarcely more comforting thought that we exist but that we cannot hope to get anywhere until we cease to exist. Alcohol, in attempting to resolve the contradiction, produces vivid patterns of Truth which vanish like snow in the morning sun and cannot be recalled; the revelations of poetry are as wonderful as a comet in the skies—and as mysterious. Love, which was once believed to contain the Answer, we now know to be nothing more than an inherited behavior pattern.

II

Before we can pronounce any judgments on Man's destiny, we must have a peek at the dilemma into which he has got himself. We must examine his nature before we can measure his hope of Heaven.

For some curious reason Man has always assumed that his is the highest form of life in the universe. There is, of course, nothing at all with which to sustain this view. Man is simply the highest form of life on his own planet. His superiority rests on a thin and chancy basis: he had the trick of articulate speech and out of this, slowly and laboriously, he developed the capacity of abstract reasoning.

Abstract reasoning, in itself, has not benefited Man so much as instinct has benefited the lower animals. On the contrary, it has moved in the opposite direction. Instinct has been defined as "a tendency to actions which lead to the attainment of some goal natural to the species." In giving up instinct and going in for reasoning, Man has aspired higher than the attainment of natural goals; he has developed ideas and notions; he has monkeyed with concepts. The life to which he was naturally adapted he has put behind him; in moving into the alien and complicated sphere of Thought and Imagination he has become the least well-adjusted of all creatures of the earth and, hence, the most bewildered. It may be that the finer mysteries of life and death can be comprehended only through pure instinct; the cat, for example, appears to Know (I don't say that he does, but he appears to). Man, on the other hand, is surely further away from the Answer than any other animal this side of the ladybug. His mistaken selection of reasoning as an instrument of perception has put him into a fine quandary.

The survival of almost any species of social animal, no matter how low, has been shown to be dependent on Group Co-operation, which is itself a product of instinct. Man's co-operative processes are jumpy, incomplete, and temporary, because they are the product of reasoning and are thus divorced from the sanity which informs all natural laws. The lower animals co-operate in the interest of the preservation of their species. Man no longer has the natural, earthy sense which would interest him in the preservation of his species. The co-operation of the lower social animals is constructive; that of man, destructive.

"Group struggles to the death between animals of the same species, such as occur in human warfare, can hardly be found among non-human animals," says W. C. Allee in his enormously interesting *The Social Life of Animals.*

The animals that depend on instinct have an inherent knowledge of the laws of economics and of how to apply them; Man, with his powers of reason, has reduced economics to the level of a farce which is at once funnier and more tragic than *Tobacco Road.* One has but to observe a community of beavers at work in a stream to understand the loss in sagacity, balance, co-operation, competence, and purpose which Man has suffered since he rose up on his hind legs. His grip on the earth and its realities began to lessen in that hour; he could walk but he had lost the opposability of his hallux, and his feet were no longer prehensile. Two of his parts increased enormously in size: his gluteus maximus and his cerebrum. He began to chatter and he developed Reason, Thought, and Imagination, qualities which would get the smartest group of rabbits or orioles in the world into inextricable trouble overnight.

Man, the aloof animal, has deteriorated in everything except mentality, and in that he has done no more than barely hold his own for the past two thousand years. He no longer understands the ways of the lower animals, and they no longer understand the ways of Man. Here again it is Man that has suffered the loss.

Next to reasoning, the greatest handicap to the optimum development of Man lies in the fact that his planet is just barely habitable. Its minimum temperatures are too low, and its maximum temperatures too high. Its day is not long enough, and its night is too long. The disposition of its water and its earth is distinctly unfortunate (the existence of the Mediterranean Sea in the place where we find it is perhaps the unhappiest accident in the whole firmament). These factors encourage depression, fear, war, and lack of vitality. They describe a planet which is by no means perfectly devised for the nurturing or for the perpetuation of a higher intelligence.

JAMES THURBER

The effect of all this on Man is everywhere apparent. On his misfit globe he has outlasted the mammoth and the pterodactyl but he has never got the upper hand of bacteria and the insects.

"This is not even the age of Man, however great his superiority in size and intelligence," writes Mr. Allee, "it is literally the age of insects."

It is surely not going too far, in view of everything, to venture the opinion that Man is not so high as he thinks he is. It is surely permissible to hazard the guess that somewhere beyond Betelgeuse there may be a race of men whose intelligence makes ours seem like the works of an old-fashioned music box. The Earth, it seems to me, may well be the Siberia or the Perth Amboy of the inhabited planets of the Universe.

III

Now that we have got Man down on his back, so to speak, let us look at the tongue of his intellect and feel the pulse of his soul.

There is a great deal to be said for his intellect, in spite of the fact that it is unquestionably coated. It has produced Genius, and out of Genius has come Art—the one achievement of Man which has made the long trip up from all fours seem well advised. Most of the faint intimations of immortality of which we are occasionally aware would seem to arise out of Art or the materials of Art.

This brings us to God and Heaven, the last stop which this exploration into the known and the unknown shall make.

Everybody is supposed to have some opinion as to whether there is life after death. Intelligent persons are expected to formulate "an integrated and consistent attitude toward life or reality"; this is known as "a philosophy" (definition 2c in *Webster's International Dictionary*).

Unfortunately, I have never been able to maintain a consistent attitude toward life or reality or toward anything else. This may be owing entirely to nervousness. At any rate, my attitudes change with the years, sometimes with the hours. Just now I am going through one of those periods when I believe that the black panther and the cedar waxwing have higher hopes of Heaven than Man has.

The dignity of Man and the Divine Destiny of Man are two things which it is at the moment impossible for me to accept with whole-hearted enthusiasm. Human Dignity has gleamed only now and then and here and there, in lonely splendor, throughout the ages, a hope of the better men, never an achievement of the majority. That which is only sporadically realized can scarcely be called characteristic. It is impossible to think of it as innate; it could never be defined as normal. Nothing is more depressing than the realization that nobility, courage, mercy, and almost all the other virtues which go to make up the ideal of Human Dignity are, at their clearest and realest, the outgrowth of Man's inhumanity to Man, the fruit of his unending interspecific struggle. The pattern is easily traceable, from Christ to Cavell.

In spite of everything, it is perhaps too easy to figure Man as merely an animal of the earth whose cerebrum developed extraordinarily, like the peacock's tail or the giraffe's neck, and to let it go at that. There is always Browning's "grand Perhaps." If it is hard to Believe, it is just as hard, as our poet's Bishop Blougram points out to the cynical Mr. Gigadibs, to "guard our unbelief." You remember: "Just when we are safest, there's a sunset-touch, a fancy from a flower-bell," and all that sort of thing—and we believe again. And then there's a man with a little mustache, and a man with an umbrella, and all *that* sort of thing, and we are safe once more in our conviction that there can be no God watching over this sorrowful and sinister scene, these menacing and meaningless animals.

We come back, in the end, to all that we can safely feel we know: A monkey-man in the eolithic times, wandering through the jungle, came upon a jewel and stuck it into his head. Since that day his descendants have given off light, sometimes a magic and blinding light. The question whether the jewel was carelessly flung off from a whirling star or carefully planned and placed by a supernatural hand has engaged the interest of mankind for a million years. The question will go on and on: Is this light a proof of God or is it no more remarkable than the plumage of a bird of paradise?

"Come, come, it's best believing, if we can," says the jovial Sylvester Blougram, over his wine. "Why not," he asks, "the Way, the Truth, the life'?"

Why not, indeed? "It is all right with me," I say over my wine. But what is all this fear of and opposition to Oblivion? What is the matter with the soft Darkness, the Dreamless Sleep?

JAMES THURBER

"Well, folks," the cheery guard may say, as the train rushes silently into a warm, dark tunnel and stops, "Here we are at good old Oblivion! Everybody out!"

"Come, come—what is the matter with that?" I ask, over my Scotch and soda.

A Biographical Sketch
of James Thurber

BY JAMES THURBER

James Thurber was born in Columbus, Ohio, where so many awful things happened to him, on December 8, 1894. He was unable to keep anything on his stomach until he was seven-years old but grew to be 6 feet 1 1/4 inches tall and to weigh a hundred and fifty-four fully dressed for winter. He began to write when he was ten-years old ("Horse Sandusky, the Intrepid Scout") and to draw when he was fourteen. He has not worked as a cow-puncher, ranch-hand, steve-dore, short-order cook, lumberjack, or preliminary prizefighter. Quick to arouse, he is very hard to quiet and people often just go away. Fond of rifle shooting but unable to concentrate, he usually fires the gun off into the air when handing it to the next marksman.

He was recently blackballed when brought up for membership in the Fairfield County (Conn.) Skeet Shooting Club. He has never been defeated at singles in crochinole. At Buckeye Lake, Ohio, in 1923 he won a canary bird throwing baseballs at dolls. He can hold a grand slam hand in contract and be set six, but he has never been taken at fan-tan. He uses the Thurber over-bidding convention and even the most skillful partners have no chance with him. He never listens when anybody else is talking, preferring to keep his mind a blank until they get through so he can talk. His favorite book is *The Great Gatsby*. His favorite author is Henry James. He wears excellent clothes very badly and can never find his hat. Two overcoats which he left in the *New Yorker* office last spring were stolen, or else he left them someplace else. He is Sagittarius with the moon in Aries and gets along fine with persons born between the 20th and the 24th of August.

JAMES THURBER

Notes

Provided here is information regarding each written piece's original date and place of publication. For some entries, pertinent items are included to elucidate allusions and contexts and to draw attention to related writings by Thurber.

Preface

xvii [BRANDON] Henry Brandon. *As We Are.* Garden City, N.Y.: Doubleday, 1961. "The Tulle and Taffeta Rut: A Conversation with James Thurber," pp. 257–82.

1 [ILLUSTRATION] *Life,* January 29, 1940.

"James Thurber Finds Revising His Play for Broadway Is 'A Great Ordeal.'" *New York World-Telegram and Sun,* January 7, 1940.

> [It represents] myself, Shumlin and Nugent working on [*The Male Animal*'s] last-minute revisions and being bothered, nonplussed, and dismayed by three concentric circles of troubles. An old lady and the muses are bothering me with ideas for dialogue, Shumlin is receiving directions from a gamin and a policeman's horse, Nugent is getting some valuable hints from the policeman himself. These represent the creatures who drift into rehearsals.
>
> Just above them, beginning with the man on the left raising his hand and ending with the man on the right holding his head, are the actors, asking if they can skip rehearsals in order to get married, falling asleep as their cue is given, requesting permission to change their lines, and suddenly being seized with a toothache.
>
> The upper circle, of course, represents the noise and clamor of New Year's. And the dogs, those rare moments of peace of mind, hope, happiness, and well-being which make it possible for authors and producer to survive the Great Ordeal.

Speaking of His Own Writing . . .

3 [LIFE] "Thurber." March 14, 1960, pp. 103–8.

3, 4, 5, 6, 7 [PARIS] Interview with George Plimpton and Max Steele. "Art of Fiction." *The Paris Review* 10 (Fall 1955), pp. 35–49.

4 [COWLEY] Malcolm Cowley. *The Literary Situation.* New York: Viking Press, 1954, pp. 189, 192.

4 [FALL AUTHOR] "James Thurber." (One of a series, "Important Authors of the Fall, Speaking for Themselves.") *New York Herald Tribune Book Review,* October 8, 1950, p. 4.

4 [GELDER] Interview with Robert Van Gelder. "Thurber's Life and Hard Times." *New York Times Book Review,* May 12, 1940, p. 20.

5, 8 [BREIT] Interview with Harvey Breit. "Mr. Thurber Observes a Serene Birthday." *New York Times Magazine,* December 4, 1949, p. 79.

6, 7 [DOLBIER] Interview with Maurice Dolbier. "A Sunday Afternoon with Mr. Thurber." *New York Herald Tribune Book Review,* November 5, 1957, p. 2.

8 From the late 1940s until the end of his life, Thurber worked at an extended piece of fiction, alternately described as a fantasy, a satire, a fairy tale, a treatment of the anxieties of the married middle-aged male, and a summing up of his anxieties about the moral and political climate of America. The project was a great pleasure and a greater frustration for Thurber, whose continual attempts were abandoned, conflated, recast, and self-pirated throughout those years with various working titles: "The Spoodle," "The Sleeping Man," "The Train on Track Six" (which Simon & Schuster announced as a forthcoming book in their listing of Spring 1955), "The Train on Track Five," "The Spoodle" (again), "The Grawk," and "The Nightinghoul."

8 In this interview of December 1949, Thurber is probably referring to the nineteenth-century saint as depicted in Frances Parkinson Keyes's *Bernadette, Maid of Lourdes* (1940), Franz Werfel's *The Song of Bernadette* (1941), or Donald Sharkey's *After Bernadette* (1945).

The Theory and Practice . . .

12 Manuscript, dated May 18, 1959. Published in the *New York Times Book Review,* December 4, 1988. These observations and objections by Thurber are modeled after a piece by Wolcott Gibbs, *The New Yorker*'s copy editor and drama critic, and, by his admission in the preface to his 1958 collection *More in Sorrow,* the man who has "contributed more words to *The New Yorker* than anybody else in its thirty-odd year span." Gibbs's letter to Harold Ross listed "a few general rules," thirty-one to be exact, to help in "bringing order out of this underbrush" of contributors and contains remarks on the treatment of dialect, adverbs, funny names, clichés, and "drunkenness and adultery," among other topics. Thurber published Gibbs's notes on editing in his own *The Years with Ross* (see pages 129–135) and adopted Gibbs's scolding, unnerved tone for his adaptation. Both pieces were probably intended as in-house memos rather than finished essays, venting frustration in the more acceptable form of offering advice. Two extended tangents from Thurber's piece are not reprinted here—one dealing with the magazine's conflicting uses of prepositions and the other with his association as a board member of *Bermudian* magazine.

12   E. B. White. *Quo Vadimus.* New York: Harper and Brothers, 1939.

13   A. E. Housman's *A Shropshire Lad,* section II, "Loveliest of trees, the cherry now . . ." The stanza reads, "Now of my three-score years and ten, / Twenty will not come again, / And take from seventy springs a score, / It only leaves me fifty more."

13   Gustave Lobrano was the fiction editor of *The New Yorker,* with whom Thurber enjoyed a productive and respectful relationship throughout his association at the magazine.

14   Thurber's reference to Coolidge's supposed remark is offered not to elucidate the idea of rejection or defeat but to show a sentence with a tautology similar to the penultimate sentence in entry 7. The quote itself is best explained by a letter to Hudson Hawley of July 27, 1954, in which Thurber describes part of his activities while working at the Paris edition of the *Chicago Tribune,* a paper that did not especially capitalize upon his talents: "I used to write parody news features mainly for the amusement of the other slaves, and one of these accidentally got sent down the chute and was set up. . . . [The editor] was always hollering up the tube for short filler items of a sentence or two, and I got away with a dozen or more phonies which were printed. The only one I remember went like this, with a Washington date line: " 'A man who does not pray is not a praying man,' President Coolidge today told the annual convention of the Protestant Churches of America.' "

15   "Big Boy," *The New Yorker,* May 4, 1929, pp. 304-7.

17   William Ernest Henley, "Echoes," section XLVII.

17   H. W. Fowler, *A Dictionary of Modern English Usage.* New York: Oxford University Press, 1965.

17   See "The Wings of Henry James" *(Lanterns and Lances)* and the present volume's "The Preface to 'The Old Friends.' "

18   "The Wings of the Falcon" was an earlier title for Thurber's piece "The Wings of Henry James," first published in *The New Yorker,* November 7, 1959.

19   The *Newsweek* article to which Thurber is probably referring is "Digest in the Doghouse," February 21, 1944.

Unfamiliar Misquotations

21   *The New Yorker,* May 20, 1939.

If You Ask Me

26   *PM*, March 17, 1941. *PM* was published by Thurber's friend Ralph Ingersoll. In *The Years with Ross,* Thurber writes: "I wrote a brief column for it . . . twice a week until I went into a nervous tailspin following my fifth eye operation. Ross read a few of these columns and objected because he said, 'You're throwing away ideas on *PM* that would make good casuals.' But I was out from under the strict and exacting editing for which *The New Yorker* was and still is famous. . . ." Indeed, Thurber did consider new and perennial ideas in thirty-three columns during 1940 and 1941. The

first twelve were illustrated and appeared with this disclaimer: "Ideas and opinions expressed in this newspaper are presented without regard to their agreement or disagreement with the editorial attitude of this writer." On January 27, 1941, an additional note accompanied the column: "James Thurber has been absent from the columns of this paper for three months, due to an eye operation. Now he is sufficiently recovered to dictate his copy to a stenographer, but he has not yet found a way to dictate Thurber drawings. His stories will appear once a week."

The illustration reprinted here publicized the column's debut and bore the following caption: "James Thurber, who for years (and years) has been writing what he feels, has turned to saying what he thinks for *PM*. His brand-new column, 'If You Ask Me,' will appear every Tuesday and Thursday, complete with opinion, guesswork, men, women, dogs and seals. (*signed*) James Thurber."

This particular essay had a subsequent appearance under the title "Writer's Age Measured by Rejection Slips" in *Parade*, September 21, 1941.

Excerpts from "The Book-End," 1923

31   *The Columbus Dispatch*, February–December 1923.

31   In 1923, as a feature writer at *The Columbus Dispatch*, Thurber wrote forty-two features entitled "Credos and Curios" in the Sunday magazine. The pages included such items as "Dad Dialogs" (exchanges on Midwestern ideals and idiocies), "The Cases of Blue Ploermell" (a parody of the popular Arthur Conan Doyle), "The Book-End" (mini-reviews and excerpts from current books), and several short bits often pertaining to events in the motion picture industry, book publishing, and the theater. The pages were illustrated with cartoons, literary portraits, and incidental drawings by Ray Evans. In many elements—note particularly the entries that engage a found piece of prose with an twist of editorial development—Thurber was developing many of the forms he would bring four years later to a new magazine called *The New Yorker*.

Rereading the columns in 1956, Thurber wrote Frank Gibney (October 31, 1956) that he felt "alarm, disbelief, and some small pleasure here and there. . . . It was practice and spadework by a man of 28 who sometimes sounds 19, praised 'clean love' and such books as *Faint Perfume* and *If Winter Comes* and practically any play or movie I saw, and attacks Cabell, Joyce, Hecht, and Sherwood Anderson. I was a great Willa Cather man."

31   James W. Faulkner, who was born in 1860 in Cincinnati and died in 1923, became one of the best-known and most respected political journalists for over thirty years in Ohio.

More Authors Cover the Snyder Trial

37   *The New Yorker*, May 7, 1927. In *The Years with Ross*, Thurber writes of reading his early submissions to the *The New Yorker*. "I marvel that Ross put his approving R on . . . a short parody called 'More Authors Cover the Snyder Trial.' In this last I tried to imitate a style of James Joyce and that of Gertrude Stein, and Ross could never have read a single line of either author. . . . In gritting his teeth, swallowing

hard, and buying that, Ross must have depended upon the counsel of his literary editor, Mrs. Katharine Angell. . . ."

In this highly publicized case, Ruth Snyder, a flapper from Queens, New York, in league with her "lover boy," Judd Gray, conspired to murder Ruth's husband, Albert, on whom Ruth had taken out a $96,000 double indemnity insurance policy. During 1926, Albert experienced seven "accidents"; on March 19, 1927, returning home from a bridge game, he was clubbed to death with a sash weight, chloroformed, and strangled with a wire. Ruth Snyder and Judd Gray were electrocuted at Sing Sing in January 1928.

If You Ask Me

39 *PM,* October 3, 1940. Besides the accompanying illustration, two added drawings hint at Thurber's discomfort with Mr. Wolfe, who "came to a party at my apartment in New York at 6 P.M. and stayed until 7 A.M. Many writers do this and I myself have no superiors in long lingering" (Letter to Neda Westlake, January 11, 1949). Several letters recount this evening of Wolfe's ravenous appetite, his "disagreeable" drunkenness, and his sense of a "real writer" as someone "whose books were so heavy they were hard to lift." Thurber wrote: "It seems that God, knowing my strength, only lets me meet great writers once: Wolfe, Lewis, Fitzgerald, Faulkner, Hemingway" (Letter to Oscar Cargill, January 14, 1953).

Recommended Reading

43 Letters to Sarah B. Whitaker, reprinted in *Alumnae News* (Northampton School for Girls), December 1962, and in the *Chicago Tribune Magazine,* May 26, 1963, under the title "James Thurber on the Perplexities of Educating a Daughter." For the present volume, only the parts of these letters that pertain to Thurber's recommended list are included. In addition, an excerpt on the same gift shelf of books from Thurber's *Bermudian* column, "Letter to the States" (December 1949), has been appended at the end of this entry.

What Price Conquest?

48 *The New Republic,* March 16, 1942. Robert Nathan (1894–1985) was a prolific and popular author in Thurber's time whose works include fantasy, children's books, poetry, plays, and fiction.

Taps at Assembly

55 *The New Republic,* February 9, 1942. In a letter of March 2, 1951, to Malcolm Cowley, the magazine's literary editor, Thurber reconsiders this review, despite "[Edmund] Wilson's note . . . saying that is was 'one of the few reviews with any critical merit' " which Thurber had shared with Cowley in a letter of February 3 the month before. "In 1941 . . . I see that I underrated the promise of that book, just as I have emotionally overstated his stature as a novelist. I have tried to see him in balance now, but the piece shows the warm admiration I will always have for him." Thurber's letter alludes to a new piece that he was writing that addressed Fitzgerald's opus as well as the Arthur Mizener biography *The Far Side of Paradise*. Thurber's finished piece, "Scott in Thorns," appears in the posthumous *Credos and Curios*.

If You Ask Me

58   *PM*, October 24, 1940.

The Odyssey *of Disney*

61   *The Nation*, March 28, 1934.

Peace, It's Wonderful

64   *The Saturday Review*, November 21, 1936. A review of *Be Glad You're Neurotic* by Louis E. Bisch, M.D. Thurber's book *Let Your Mind Alone* develops Thurber's reservations on the whole psychiatric, self-improvement subject.

66   A grim souvenir of the kidnapping of the Lindbergh baby, miniature ladders, similar to the one Hauptmann used to abscond with the child, were sold in various parts of the country.

Tempest in a Looking Glass

67   *Forum and Century*, April 1937.

Voices of Revolution

73   *The New Republic*, March 25, 1936. This piece, the following one entitled "Notes for a Proletarian Novel," and many of Thurber's letters during this period touch on Thurber's ongoing concern with the relationship of Marxism and Communism to the literary community in which he found himself: "I'm protesting, mainly, against being classed as a bourgeois who does not, cannot, know the feelings of the proletarian. That's one reason I undertook this book: I want to know, and feel at home, among these proletarian writers" (Letter to Malcolm Cowley, February 3, 1951). In this, one of several voluminous midnight letters on the subject, Thurber wrote to his friend and editor: "I have written, I suppose, at least fifty thousand words in my fifteen or twenty rewrites of this piece. I have spent at least fifty solid hours of work on the mere writing, perhaps twenty on the reading. . . . I have been influenced by nothing except my own feelings, definitely my feelings as a writer, possibly my feelings as a bourgeois (a hell of a goddam loose word to apply to all Americans who are not proletarians. After all my grandfather had a stand on Central Market and my father never made more than $50 a week in his life). . . . What is essentially the matter . . . [is that] nobody, reading this book as carefully as I have, can fail to see that these people are, for the most part, essentially writers. You feel that, as such, they would, first of all, like to have this be a Utopian world, as quickly as possible, in which it would be all right to write for *The New Yorker*. But it isn't such a world. Therefore, they go over to writing about the proletariat (about whose actions, reactions, idioms, and gestures they betray a constant pathetic ignorance) and because they *have* to do this rather than *want* to do it there arises bitterness, anger, and, of all things, this curious wail and plaint against the sex life of the bourgeois."

Notes for a Proletarian Novel

84   *The New Yorker*, June 9, 1934.

84   Stanley J. Weyman (1855–1928) published several popular books, often sub-titled "a romance," during Thurber's pre–*New Yorker* years. His works include *The Wild Geese, The Man in Black, Sophia, The Long Night,* and *Under the Red Robe.*

Ave Atque Vale

89   *Bermudian*, November 1950. When Harold Ross died, Thurber wrote his friend Ronald Williams (December 15, 1951) that he had shown E. B. White this drawing and that "he was all for using it as the illustration for the obituary, but the conservative boys turned it down. Now Andy and I have made a pledge to use it for the obituary of whichever one of us dies first. I will either write his, or he will write mine." Thurber died first. His obituary was written by White, but no drawing accompanied it. His gravestone in Columbus, Ohio, does bear a picture of "the last flower" from Thurber's book of that name.

Recollections of Henry James

91   *The New Yorker*, June 17, 1933.

The Preface to "The Old Friends"

96   Unpublished manuscript, dated 1955. Thurber's earlier parenthetical gloss affords some alternate information on this piece's occasion: "A Small Attempt to Prefigure After Re-reading Henry James's Preface to *What Maisie Knew*, the Sort of Verbal Fragment Upon Which the Master Might Have Stumbled At Almost Any Party, In This Year of Jeopardy, And What He Might Have 'Done,' As Who Should Say, With It." In his conversation with *The Paris Review*, Thurber discusses a work-in-progress "in which [Henry] James at the age of 104 writes a preface to a novel about our age in which he summarizes the trends and complications but at the end is so completely lost he doesn't really care enough to read it over to find his way out again."

In addition to his three parodies of Henry James, Thurber also wrote "A Call on Mrs. Forrester (After Re-reading, in My Middle Years, Willa Cather's *A Lost Lady* and Henry James's *The Ambassadors*)," published in *The Beast in Me;* an unpublished casual, "An Adventure in Time," an antic family episode touching on his personal relationship with Madame de Vionnet of *The Ambassadors;* and several letters detailing the possible theatrical adaptation of *The Ambassadors,* as well as other smaller tributes and discussions. Henry James also features prominently in two other pieces included in this volume: "Recollections of Henry James," a fabricated meeting with the Master, and "One Man in His Time," an imagined collaborative work by Eugene O'Neill and Henry James.

The Harpers and Their Circle

106   "Letter from the States," *Bermudian*, July 1951.

A Visit from Saint Nicholas

110   *The New Yorker*, December 24, 1927, Thurber's first Christmas at the magazine.

An Evening with Carl Sandburg

115   Included are three unpublished drawings as well as reprints of the two playing instruments and reading to one another, which did appear in *Thurber & Co.*

A letter from Sandburg, dated May 14, 1947—more than ten years after this meeting—expresses something of their shared admiration:

"It is long since that dandy all-night session in Columbus, Ohio. And you keep growing all the time, gathering a permanent audience that cherishes you as very real to them. Some of them would form James Thurber reading and study clubs and then drop the idea on hearing, 'Thurber is old-fashioned black-walnut Quaker mixed with modern-chromium philosophical anarchist and you cant [*sic*] organize it.' I started meaning to tell you Asheville amateur players put on *The Male Animal* this March and it stood forth as a classic and was a hit and you would have been proud and humble and when they hauled me before the curtain between acts I praised the players and the audience and testified that you are a clown and an architect and amid all your shenanigans a man of great faith and I wouldn't go into details about angles of you that are near heroic. May you go on."

No More Biographies

118   *The New Yorker*, March 19, 1932.

How to Tell a Fine Old Wine

121   *The New Yorker*, February 24, 1934.

What Price a Farewell to Designs?

126   *The New Yorker*, March 18, 1933.

The Literary Meet

129   *The New Yorker*, September 24, 1927. The magazine *Liberty*, along with *The Saturday Evening Post* and *Collier's*, were the three weekly miscellanies with large circulations at the time.

Memoirs of a Banquet Speaker

136   *The New Yorker*, March 29, 1930.

136   Captain George Fried, master mariner, was widely recognized for rescuing the crew members of the steamer ships *Antinoe* (January 1926) and *Florida* (January 1929).

Answers-to-Hard-Questions Department

143   *The New Yorker*, August 2, 1930.

JAMES THURBER

147   During his association with *The New Yorker,* Thurber often wrote under various pseudonyms. These included Jamie Machree; Col. Bolton Field-Field, K.C.B., V.C., M.P., K.R.G.E.; Childe Harold; James Grover; Rags; J. G. T.; T. J. G.; G. T. J.; Foot Fault (for his serial feature "The Tennis Courts"); and Jared L. Manley (for the serial "Where Are They Now?"). Of course, many of Thurber's casuals for *The New Yorker* observed the practice of "we," the magazine-as-writer, and carried no by-line.

Speaking of Drawings . . .

148   [COOKE] Interview with Alistair Cooke. (First presented on *Omnibus,* the Ford Foundation TV program.) *Atlantic Monthly,* August 1956, pp. 36–40.

148   [GARLAND] James Thurber. *A Thurber Garland.* London: Hamish Hamilton, 1955, Preface.

149   [DE VRIES] Letter to Peter De Vries, October 16, 1952.

149   [SHER] Interview with Jack Sher. "Meet James Thurber." *Detroit Free Press Sunday Magazine,* February 25, 1940, p. 23.

150   [GUMP] Letter to S. and G. Gump Art Gallery, reprinted in article by Emilia Hodel in the *San Francisco News,* March 6, 1937.

152   [MILLER] Letter to Herman Miller, undated (1940).

153   [ROSS] Letter to Harold Ross, October 20, 1941, published in *Thurber, A Biography* by Burton Bernstein. New York: Dodd, Mead, 1975.

153   The three drawings in the October 18 issue of *The New Yorker* to which Thurber refers are by Richard Decker, Alan Dunn, and Ned Hilton, respectively.

Glimpses of the Art Conference

157   In *The Years with Ross,* Thurber alludes to these drawings: "I once made a series of drawings especially for Ross about the trials and tortures of the art meeting. One showed the scowling Ross himself shoving a drawing at a timid office employee and snarling, 'Is that funny?' . . . Two of the other art meeting drawings I did for Ross ('You tease him too much,' my mother once told me sternly. 'You shouldn't tease him so much.') showed, respectively, an old woman asking for a cup of cold water at a storage dam, and the same old woman asking a fireman for a match at a great conflagration. The editor had the drawings framed and hung on the walls of his office to remind him of the threat of formula."

Tonight at 8:30

164   *Stage,* December 1936. Thurber contributed several illustrated comments to this theater publication, including pieces on *A Day at the Races* (see present volume under "Groucho and Me"), George White's *Scandals,* Mae West's *Klondike Annie,* a theatrical revival of *Pride and Prejudice,* and Katharine Dayton and George S. Kaufman's *First Lady.* The illustrations in "James Thurber Presents William Shake-

speare" that are collected in *Thurber & Company* were another part of his *Stage* contribution.

Letter from the States

169 *Bermudian*, April 1950.

A Farewell to Santa Claus

173 *The New Yorker*, December 24, 1932. Reprinted in the *New York Times*, December 24, 1988.

One Man in His Time

179 *The New Yorker*, January 20, 1934.

Is There a Killer in the House?

184 *The Observer* (London), July 10, 1955.

Producers Never Think Twice

190 *The New Yorker*, February 16, 1935.

Roaming in the Gloaming

194 *New York Times*, January 7, 1940.

The Quality of Mirth

201 This speech, originally given at the London opening of *A Thurber Carnival* at the ANTA, was printed in the Sunday *New York Times*, February 21, 1960. Among James Thurber's papers is a brief annotation for a section called "Matinee and Evening." It remains unclear whether this was a book's section planned by Thurber himself or by his wife, Helen, who brought out the posthumous volumes *Thurber & Company, Credos and Curios,* and *Selected Letters of James Thurber.* The note suggested the following cluster: "On the Brink of Was," "The Quality of Mirth," "The State of Humor in the States," and "The Other Side of the Footlights."

And the World Laughs with Them

207 *The New Yorker*, September 29, 1934.

Groucho and Me

213 *New York Herald Tribune Book Review*, September 13, 1959. While photographs from Marx's *Groucho and Me* originally accompanied this review, included here are portraits of the Marx Brothers taken from an article by Teet Carle that appeared in *Stage*, March 1937. Thurber illustrated Carle's "Laughing Stock, Common and Preferred" and contributed the small prose feature and illustration that appears after the review.

JAMES THURBER

Speaking of Humor . . .

217 [EASTMAN] Max Eastman. *Enjoyment of Laughter.* New York: Simon & Schuster, 1936, p. 341.

218, 220 [LANDAU] Two letters to Elliott D. Landau, June 9, 1954, June 25, 1954, reprinted in *Horn Book Magazine,* "Quibble, Quibble: Funny? Yes; Humorous, No!" April 1962, pp. 162–64.

220 A. E. Housman's *Last Poems,* section II, "As I gird on for fighting . . ." Its last stanza reads: "So here are things to think on/That ought to make me brave,/As I strap on for fighting/My sword that will not save."

221 [SMALL WORLD] "That Girl in Galway." *New York Post,* March 25, 1959. (A transcript of Thurber, Noel Coward, and actress Siobhan McKenna on Ed Murrow's CBS TV show "Small World.")

221 [COWLEY LETTER] Letter to Malcolm Cowley, March 11, 1954.

222 [BUCHWALD] "A Letter from James Thurber About Art Buchwald's *More Caviar.*" *New York Times,* April 16, 1959, p. 35.

222 [BREIT–2] Interview with Harvey Breit. "Talk with James Thurber." *New York Times Book Review,* June 29, 1952, p. 19.

223 [TIME] " 'The Time of Your Life' Is Now." *New York World-Telegram and Sun,* August 21, 1961, p. 4. (Written for the Associated Press and printed under various titles in papers nationwide.)

The State of Humor in the States

226 *New York Times,* September 4, 1960.

How to Tell Government from Show Business

231 This unpublished manuscript was written in London during performances of *A Thurber Carnival* and, according to a note, was "revised March 20, 1961."

On the Brink of Was

234 *New York Times Magazine,* December 7, 1958. Thurber's reply, along with statements by Mort Sahl, Al Capp, Jerry Lewis, and Steve Allen, appeared in a forum entitled "State of the Nation's Humor."

Thinking Ourselves into Trouble

240 *Forum and Century,* June 1939, as well as in the collection *I Believe: The Personal Philosophies of Certain Eminent Men and Women of Our Time,* edited by Clifton Fadiman. New York: Simon & Schuster, 1939.

List of Illustrations

Drawings that appeared as illustrations to Thurber's own work are listed in the Notes and are not given additional mention here.

Cover   This illustration, "Thurber and Nugent at Work on The Male Animal," appeared in a popular AP story by Jack Stinnett, which ran among other places in *The Washington Star,* February 25, 1940.

Illustration on binding   [Man with dog resting on his knee] *The New Yorker,* December 31, 1938.

Endpapers   "In the millennium men will not cease to be men." *Books,* April 30, 1939.

Frontispiece   Illustration of James Thurber by Marc Simont.

Title page   [Man and girl fighting over book] Advertisement by Harper & Brothers for *Fables for Our Time,* in *The New Yorker,* October 5, 1940.

xii   "Fig. I, Zeiss Loop" and holograph page, from a letter to Herman and Dorothy Miller, May 23, 1943.

1   [Thurber at desk with a sky of figures] From "Thurber Finds Revising His Play for Broadway Is 'A Great Ordeal.'" *New York World-Telegram,* January 7, 1940.

9   "Do you ever have fears that you may cease to be before your pen has gleaned your teeming brain?" *The New Yorker,* October 2, 1943.

10   "He's giving Dorothy Thompson a piece of his mind." *The New Yorker,* May 16, 1939.

11   "Courting the Muse?" *The Saturday Review,* December 14, 1935.

24   "It's nothing serious, Madam. They're writers." *The Saturday Review,* December 17, 1938.

25 "8 Important Characters in James Thurber's New Column." *New York Times,* September 19, 1940.

29 [Woman writing, with man and dog looking on] Cover for *The Pocket Entertainer,* Shirley Cunningham, ed. New York: Pocket Books, 1942.

36 "Am I the only woman in America who isn't writing novels?" *The Saturday Review,* April 15, 15, 1939.

39 [Man at desk with dog staring at him] *PM,* October 3, 1940; also *Thurber and Company.*

41 "This is my house, Mr. Wolfe, and if you don't get out I'll throw you out!" *New York Herald Tribune,* March 9, 1947 (from a feature on Thurber drawings in Costello's Saloon, New York).

42 "He looks a little like Thomas Wolfe, and he certainly makes the most of it." *The New Yorker,* November 23, 1935.

52 "I told Womrath's I don't want to read anything instructive until the war ends." *The New Yorker,* October 14, 1944.

53 "Your faith is really more disturbing than my atheism." *The New Yorker,* March 23, 1946.

54 "Professor Townsend is really too high-strung to be a philosopher." *The New Yorker,* January 23, 1943.

78 "This is my brother Ed. He's given up." *The New Yorker,* September 1, 1934.

79 " 'Don'ts' for the Inflation." *The New Yorker,* March 18, 1933.

103 [The Reading Hour] *Thurber & Company.*

105 "There isn't room in this house for belles lettres and me both." *Saturday Review,* November 5, 1938.

113 "Ravel's 'Bolero.' " Unpublished.

114 "Folks out of Faulkner." Unpublished.

115 [Thurber and Sandburg playing guitars] *Thurber & Company.*

116 "Dance Recital." Unpublished.

116 [Thurber dancing with Carl Sandburg] Unpublished.

117 "Sandburg Tells a Story." Unpublished.

117 "Jeez, it <u>looks</u> like Sandburg's plane, don't it?" Unpublished.

122 [Waiter serving diners] Part of an ad for the French Line, *The New Yorker,* June 10, 1933.

131 "How is it possible, woman, in the awful and magnificent times we live in, to be preoccupied exclusively with the piddling?" *The New Yorker,* February 16, 1946.

132 "I want to send that one about 'Instead of hearts and cupid's darts I'm sending you a wire,' or whatever the hell it is!" *The New Yorker,* February 11, 1933.

133 "The trouble is you make me think too much." *The New Yorker,* April 25, 1942.

134 "Well, *I* call it Carib<u>bb</u>ean, and I intend to go to my grave calling it Carib<u>b</u>ean." *The New Yorker,* January 29, 1944.

135 "Hey, Joe. How d'ya spell 'rhythm'?" *The New Yorker,* September 16, 1933.

141 [Thurber, hand on dog's head] *New York Times,* March 1, 1931.

151 "Mr. Sandusky" and "nameless candidate," drawings from an unpublished, undated letter to Herman Miller, which appeared in the *Ladies' Home Journal,* July 1946.

152 "Hm. Explorers." A redrawing of the first drawing Thurber ever submitted to *The New Yorker. Ladies' Home Journal,* July 1946.

157 "The Art Conference discovers the work of R. Taylor." Unpublished, collection of the Ohio State University.

158 "The Art Conference decides the Dust Bowl is not known to *New Yorker* readers." Unpublished, collection of the Ohio State University.

158 The funny picture is rejected because you can't tell who is talking, the old lady or the fireman, and because we had a picture of a man trying to get a drink at a dam. Besides, how did the old lady get through the police lines?" Unpublished, collection of *The New Yorker.* Copyright by *The New Yorker* Magazine, Inc. All rights reserved.

159 "The Art Conference buys its one hundredth drawing of 3 people on a tiny island." Unpublished, collection of the Ohio State University.

159 "Midsummer Art Conference." Unpublished, collection of *The New Yorker.* Copyright by *The New Yorker* Magazine, Inc. All rights reserved.

160 The Outside Opinion: 'Is That Funny?' " Unpublished, collection of *The New Yorker.* Copyright by *The New Yorker* Magazine, Inc. All rights reserved.

160 "Art Conference: Ceiling Zero." Unpublished, collection of the Ohio State University.

161 [Seated woman and others, arguing] Cover for *Theatre Arts Magazine,* March 1940.

163 "The astonished hands were dancing across the family fumed heart." *Stage,* December 1936.

168 Tableau from *Tonight at 8:30. Stage,* December 1936.

176 "I had the strangest feeling in the elevator that I was changing into Clare Luce." *The New Yorker,* May 22, 1943.

177 "Well, I've found Miss Gish for you, Mr. Freeman. No relation to the sisters, incidentally." *The New Yorker,* May 9, 1936.

JAMES THURBER

About the Author

Born in Columbus, Ohio, in 1894 and buried there in 1961, James Thurber changed the face of American humor in just about thirty years and as many books. After attending the Ohio State University, where he edited the humor magazine and contributed musicals to its dramatic club, he became a newspaper reporter, working for the *Columbus Dispatch,* the *Paris Tribune* and the *New York Evening Post.* In 1927 he joined *The New Yorker* and helped shape its identity throughout its first two decades. His first book, *Is Sex Necessary?* in collaboration with E. B. White, launched a matchless career of prose and pictures that includes five children's books, two books of fables, two memoirs, two theatrical works, and eighteen anthologies of cartoons and writings.

About the Editor

Michael J. Rosen was born and reared in James Thurber's Columbus-town, and, after receiving his MFA from Columbia University, returned there to become the literary director of The Thurber House, the writer's center in James Thurber's boyhood home. His own poetry, criticism, fiction and illustrations have been supported by grants from the National Endowment for the Arts, Ingram Merrill Foundation, and Ohio Arts Council, and published in such places as *The New Yorker, Gourmet, Salmagundi, The Nation,* and *The New Criterion.* His books include *A Drink at the Mirage,* a collection of poetry, and *50 Odd Jobs,* a children's book of pictures and verses.

2939?